The Cambridge Manuals of Science and
Literature

COMPARATIVE RELIGION

COMPARATIVE RELIGION

BY

F. B. JEVONS, Litt.D.

Professor of Philosophy in the
University of Durham

Cambridge :
at the University Press

1913

CAMBRIDGE UNIVERSITY PRESS
Cambridge, New York, Melbourne, Madrid, Cape Town,
Singapore, São Paulo, Delhi, Tokyo, Mexico City

Cambridge University Press
The Edinburgh Building, Cambridge CB2 8RU, UK

Published in the United States of America by
Cambridge University Press, New York

www.cambridge.org
Information on this title: www.cambridge.org/9781107401754

© Cambridge University Press 1913

First published 1913
First paperback edition 2011

A catalogue record for this publication is available from the British Library

ISBN 978-1-107-40175-4 Paperback

*With the exception of the coat of arms
at the foot, the design on the title page is a
reproduction of one used by the earliest known
Cambridge printer, John Siberch, 1521*

PREFACE

THE attitude a man takes towards God, or the idea
of God, is of fundamental importance for himself ;
and he is therefore naturally interested in knowing
what is the attitude taken up by others who, being
men, are like himself. So far as he knows it, or
surmises it, he cannot help comparing it with his
own attitude : he has started on the Method of
Comparison, and he cannot help seeing both resemblances and differences between his own attitude
and that of others. Having started, he may or
may not go on ; but, if he stops short, his comparisons
will not be of much value to himself or anybody
else : the Comparative Method must take into
account all the facts, or else it will be misleading.
Nothing human can be wholly without interest for
any man, or without its lesson for him, if he has
intelligence and sympathy ; and the more sympathy
and intelligence he has, the deeper will be his interest.
From the study of Comparative Religion, that is,
from the study of the attitude taken towards God
in the religions of the world, he may learn something of the deepest interest, if he has any sympathy
with his fellow-man. He may start with the opinion,

and may be confirmed in his opinion, that religions differ widely from one another. But, in that case, he will also learn the resemblance they have through all their differences. The object the study of Comparative Religion has is not so much to ascertain what we men think as what we feel and how we act. It is the study of one way—not the least important or least interesting way—in which our personality expresses itself.

F. B. JEVONS.

HATFIELD HALL, DURHAM,
13*th November* 1912.

CONTENTS

COMPARATIVE RELIGION

CHAPTER I

INTRODUCTION

THE problem of the relation of men to their gods is
one which men at all times of their history have
been engaged in endeavouring to work out by the
practical method of experiment. The experiments
have been, and still are, very various. They are the
numerous religions which exist or have existed.

But various as they are—and each one differs
from every other—they have their resemblances
to one another. It is because they have their
resemblances and their differences that it is possible
to compare them. It is their resemblance in their
difference, and their differences in their resemblance
that makes it necessary to study them by the
Comparative Method, or the method of Comparative
Religion. In employing the Comparative Method
there is a danger—the danger of thinking that the
object and purpose of comparison is to ascertain
merely the points of likeness between the various
religions of the world. To think so, however, is to

A   1

overlook the plain fact that for scientific purposes
the differences which the Comparative Method
reveals are just as important, and, scientifically,
as valuable, as the resemblances. In Comparative
Philology the differences between the languages
compared are from the scientific point of view as
fundamentally important as the resemblances ;
and in practical life it is the unlikeness between
your own language and another which makes all
the difference. Doubtless, too, you speak your
own language all the better for knowing another,
and think the more clearly : you are less liable to
fall a victim to verbal fallacies and forms of speech.

The relation of men to their gods is a problem
which men are and have been engaged in working
out practically. In the case of those peoples,
therefore, who have a recorded history, we have a
historical record of the way in which they have
worked at it. They are the civilised peoples of
the world. The peoples who have no recorded,
documentary history are the uncivilised peoples
of the earth. But these, though they have no
history, recorded in documents, have a past : they
are just as far removed in time from the beginnings
of mankind as are the most civilised of their con-
temporaries. We may surmise their past ; we may
even re-construct it inferentially. But such surmises and re-constructions are less trustworthy

and less valuable than the information afforded to us by the documents and records of the past which have been preserved by the civilised peoples. These records are first in importance, if we wish to ascertain the way in which, as a matter of fact, men have worked and are working at the problem of the relation of men to their gods.

Religions with a recorded history may be divided into two classes. In one class we may place those which no longer exist—the religions of ancient Egypt, of the Babylonians and Assyrians, of the classical Greeks and Romans, and of the Teutons. In the other class we may place those which are still living, active faiths—the religions of the Chinese, the Jews, the Vedic and Brahministic religion, Hinduism, Mahommedanism, Buddhism, Christianity. Religions having no recorded history are those found in Africa, amongst the aborigines of America, Australia, the South Sea, and the Mongols.

Self-preservation is, in a sense, the first law of nature. It is first in the sense that, unless it is complied with, there is an end, in this life at any rate, to the individual, animal or human, that fails to comply with it. Compliance with it is the condition without which no other or further activity is possible. It is the first law of nature also in the sense that most people do act on it ; though it is generally recognised that there are occasions on which, and persons with whom, it is rightly not the first thing to be taken into account. Against the dangers which do or may threaten him man protects himself as best he may. Whether man was or was not originally a gregarious animal, he found protection, originally or eventually, from many dangers, by living in communities ; and, by the co-operation and the division of labour which ensued, he gained many positive advantages. Defence of the community was self-defence ; and its preservation, self-preservation. Of some of the dangers which threatened, or of the calamities which afflicted, the community or the individual, the authors were obvious ; but of many, mysterious. With these mysterious authors of calamity it was the affair of the community to deal, if it was the community that suffered ; and the affair of the individual to deal, if it was on him that the calamity fell.

For the calamity which befalls the community, it was, and indeed is, felt that there must be some reason ; and the reason, generally accepted both in the less and the more developed religions of the world, is that the calamity is a visitation from some being or power. In the more highly evolved religions of peoples having a recorded history behind them, such beings or powers are gods, bearing personal names and having a personal history. In the less highly evolved religions of peoples having no historical records, the being or power who sends the calamity and visits the people may have no personal name or history. And it is obvious that in the history of the more developed religions there must have been a stage when their gods also had as yet acquired no personal names and had achieved no personal history. A calamity, then, which befalls the community is regarded as a visitation from some being or power, conceived as personal—vaguely conceived in the earlier stages, and more definitely personal in the later stages. From this visitation the community wishes to be relieved ; and on behalf of the community the head-man may, and in some cases known to us does, simply request the power who has brought the calamity to go away, and offerings are made to induce him to go away. But, as nothing happens without a reason, neither could this being, vaguely conceived as personal, have visited the community without a reason ; and, as he visited them with calamity, his reason must have been that he was offended with them, and by something that some member of the community had done. The offence in question must have been some departure from the ordinary custom of the community, some transgression of what was felt by the community to be forbidden, some violation of taboo. Thus the things which the community feel to be forbidden or taboo are interpreted as being things forbidden by the vaguely personal power who has visited the community with calamity. In China, " the infliction of plague, pestilence and famine is traced to Heaven's displeasure in consequence of national disobedience."

Thus far we have been concerned with the calamities which befell a community, and which it concerned the community to stay, if possible. But there are calamities which may befall the individual alone, such as sickness or death ; and against which it is the business of the individual or those personally interested in him to provide. These individual misfortunes also have their authors, for whom search must be made, if the reason for the misfortunes is to be removed. And search is made ; but, as it is made on behalf of the suffering individual and not on behalf of the community by the headman, it is not an affair of the community, but a private affair. Thus one difference between magic and most forms of religion is manifest : magic is an affair of individuals, religion of the community. Further, the sickness or death of an individual is, in the more backward stages of culture, generally ascribed to the malevolent action of some human being ; and the person credited, or rather debited, with the offence is a person who is marked out, by some peculiarity of appearance, manner or character, as the sort of person who in the opinion of the community would be likely—both able and willing —to work mischief. The suggestion that a person has this power is apt to lead the person to believe that he has the power, and to attempt to exercise it. He stands to gain in various ways by exercising his power ; and he proceeds—in the opinion of the community—to exercise it. It is probably on human beings that he is first believed to exercise it ; but he may also proceed to exercise it on beings other than human. In the penitential psalms from the library of Ashurbanipal, the Babylonian worshipper complains to his god of the ill-success of the magician whom he called to his assistance : "The magician did not unloose by a charm the curse upon me. The exorcist has not handled my illness successfully ; nor has the diviner set a termination to my malady." Here, in Babylonia, magic or counter-magic has accommodated itself —as it did in ancient Egypt also—to the national religion, and is tolerated by its side. But usually magic, as being exercised by individuals, generally for purposes harmful to the community, is felt to be offensive to the gods of the community and is condemned as irreligious. This condemnation, however, is probably weak and ineffective so long as the community itself, when visited by tribal afflictions, gets no further than making offerings and begging the author of the calamity simply to go away. Even at this stage, however, the difference is fairly obvious between the man who works magic or counter-magic, controlling human beings or spirits by means of his personal power, and the community which through its head-man begs that the visitation of calamity may be removed.

We have not, however, yet exhausted the list of the possible sources of the calamity and afflictions which befall man. There yet remain ghosts, and the spirits of the departed. The geographical distribution of ghosts is quite as wide as that of gods or magicians. And whether the appearance of ghosts is followed by calamity, or not, their appearance is in itself terrifying ; and the normal—probably the earliest—practical step that is taken is to try to induce them to go away. That seems to be the purpose of most funerary ceremonials.

The possible sources, then, of mysterious calamity to the individual and the community were three : the perturbed spirits of the dead, the malevolent and magical power of living persons, and the offended power of mysterious personalities. The reason of the calamities brought on the individual by or through the action of magicians and witches was found in the ill-will of some living individual. The reason of the calamities brought on the community from the other two sources was found in the conviction that some departure had been made from the ordinary course of things, from the custom of the community. This departure from the custom of the community may be described as a violation of taboo, or as a transgression of the customary morality of the tribe. To depart from the custom was felt to be a forbidden thing. Hence it is that all early systems of morality present themselves in the negative form of prohibitions: " thou shalt not." Hence, too, in all early forms of religion, calamity to the community is regarded as a visitation from some being offended by a departure from custom, that is from the customary morality of the tribe. Man brings calamity on himself, and brings it by doing that which is taboo, by violating custom, by transgressing morality.

The offended being or power may be supplicated simply to depart, and offerings may be made to him to induce him to go away. But they may be renewed in order to induce him to stay away ; and, as a matter of fact, sacrifices to the gods and festivals of the dead are found everywhere to recur at regular seasons. By the time, however, that this is brought about, and probably in part owing to the fact that it does come about, a change or a development in the relations of the community to these powers gradually takes place. When the making of offerings has established itself as part of the custom of the community, the beings to whom they are offered have come to establish themselves in the consciousness of the community. They are no longer strangers, still less are they hostile. If calamity does, as it will, still visit the community, the prayer of the community is no longer that the being whom they worship will depart, but that he will become reconciled to his worshippers and abate his wrath. At this point, in most of the historical religions of the world, a distinction manifests itself in the consciousness of the community between the spirits of the dead and the other beings to whom the community makes offerings. The spirits of the dead are besought not only to go away but to stay away : the fact that they return, as ghosts or in dreams, is regarded as abnormal, as a departure from the custom of the dead, and as a departure which can be accounted for on the supposition that they have not received due rites of burial. Thus the rites of burial due to them come to be regarded as a means of keeping the spirits of the dead from interfering with the living. From the spirits of the dead the living may have something to fear ; they have little or nothing to hope. It is to the beings worshipped by the community that the community turns for aid and the gratification of their desires, or the satisfaction of their needs. But though this line of evolution which led away from the worship

of ancestors was the line followed by the ancient
Egyptians, the Babylonians, and Assyrians, the
Israelites, the ancient Persians, and—though for a
different reason—by the Buddhists, still, as religion
has no one line of evolution but each religion follows
its own course, we find, pre-eminently amongst the
Chinese, and to a less extent amongst most of the
Indo-European peoples in the past, that the spirits
of deceased ancestors as well as the gods are the
objects of cult ; and, though the purpose of the
ancestral cult is primarily to avert calamity, it may
also be to obtain earthly blessings.

Generally we may say that the calamities which
befall the community are regarded as visitations
due to the fact that there has been, on the part of
some member or other, a departure from the custom,
or customary morality, of the community ; and
that offerings are made to the offended power or
deity, to make atonement, to stay his wrath, and to
effect a reconciliation. The fall of the tower of
Siloam is interpreted as the visitation for sin committed by some one. Natural as such an interpretation is, so long as we start from the position
that man brings worldly calamity on himself by
transgression, by doing that which, on the customary morality of the community, he should not do,
still it is remarkable that most of the great historical
religions should have concerned themselves much

more with expiating offences and placating their deities, by means of offerings and sacrifices, than with seeking to eradicate the offences themselves. The latter means—the means of avoidance—was that which was taught by Buddha : avoid transgressions of the customary morality ; abstain, not merely from offences, but from the desires which lead inevitably to them ; abstain from the desire which is the root of all offences, the desire to live ; and the very possibility of offence is removed. This doctrine is the consummation of the negative attitude in religion and morality—the negative attitude of taboo, of the morality which confines itself to prohibitions and says " thou shalt not," and of the religions which base themselves on fear. It is the logical issue—which is perhaps the reason why it was not more often drawn—and, pressed home consistently, it is the logical destruction of religious and moral systems so far as they are built on a negative, that is are based on nought. Where gods are postulated merely for the sake of punishing transgressions, avoidance of transgressions leaves them void of functions—empty postulates—as Buddha saw. If Buddha has himself come to be worshipped as a god, it is not because he punishes transgressions, it is because his followers' idea of God contained something more than Buddha's logical analysis of it revealed. The tacit assumption of Buddha's teaching, the basis unexpressed in positive words, was that the idea of God is unnecessary. The history of Buddhism, however, shows that the idea of God proves indispensable.

Another attempt—which also failed—to dispense with the idea of a personal god is afforded by the teaching of Zarathustra in ancient Persia. To understand it we must start once more from the fact that calamities befall men, both individual men and communities of men; and that they are regarded as the doing of personalities, more or less vaguely conceived. Calamities may be due to the action of magicians, of the spirits of the deceased, or of some power or being, conceived as personal; and it may be averted from coming, or withdrawn when it has come, if the power that causes it is properly approached. The assumption made is that the author of the calamity is placable and will withdraw the calamity, if the cause of his wrath is removed. He is not regarded as simply and inherently malevolent. A magician, or the person who employs him, may be malevolent; and so, too, may be the ghost of a malevolent person. Whether the beings other than living men and the spirits of the dead are inherently malevolent is a question which is not to be settled a priori, but only after an attempt to appease them has been made. If the attempt succeeds, the being is shown to be placable and comes in due time to be worshipped. If that attempt does not succeed, such beings are shown to be, of their nature, malevolent, and hostile in their action.

It was this circle of ideas that Zarathustra, a priest of the fire-god, found in existence. There were powers, hostile, malevolent, and therefore wicked ; and there were powers, like that of the sacred fire, which were essentially powers of purity, of purification from uncleanness, and of righteousness. It was the antagonism of these two principles of wickedness and righteousness that constituted, in Zarathustra's teaching, the whole world-process. His doctrine was of a dualism of principles ; and the good power is, in the Gāthas, envisaged rather as a principle than as a person : Ahura Mazda is not a proper, or personal, name ; it is simply " wisdom." But the Persians found it impossible to remain satisfied with a principle, in the place of a personal god ; and the introduction of Mithra and Anahita at any rate personalised Ahura Mazda, even though in so doing it precipitated Zarathustra's abstract principles into a form of polytheism.

Thus far we have been concerned with the relation of men to their gods in this life ; and the justification for so confining ourselves, if justification be required, is to be found in the fact that so many of the historical religions of the world have confined themselves, either in the beginning or throughout their history, to the relation of men to their gods in this life. That " in the grave men do not praise Thee " was the conviction not only of the Israelites, but of the Greeks and Romans until the appearance amongst them of the mysteries, and of the Babylonians and Assyrians throughout, as it is to the present day of the Chinese and the various Hindoo sects. The dead are the departed, and the living are concerned only to prevent their ghosts from returning. Speculation as to the state and condition of the departed does not—for whatever reason—flourish. Belief in the transmigration of souls, again, which is found in Brahminism and Buddhism, does not carry us beyond this world : for it is in other human forms, or animal, in this world that the transmigrating soul re-appears. It was in ancient Egypt and Persia, first, that the relation of men to their gods in the next life became an object of attention. Later, in Buddhism, if not in Buddha's teaching, Nirvāna became a state of conscious and blessed existence ; and, in Mahommedanism and Christianity, the next life—differently conceived in the two cases—plays an important part in this.

In all the religions of the world the relation of men to their gods is regarded in the first instance as being a relation of the community to the gods of the community. The gods protect and assist the community : the community worships the gods. Where—as in Japan and amongst the Jews—the relation is explained as having its basis in a covenant entered into, the covenant is as between the god or gods on the one hand, and the community on the other. The relation is not between the gods and any particular member of the community. Religion, in fact, was an affair of the community rather than of the individual : it was national rather than personal. This subordination of the individual personality to the community—which finds an expression in intense patriotism—is more easily maintained in a small community, such as that of the Jews or those of the Greeks later, than in a big one ; and that is probably one reason why it was in ancient Egypt, a great state, in which many political communities, originally separate, were fused, that the value of personality was first recognised, and was felt to be indestructible. In the empire of ancient Egypt, despotically ruled, there was opportunity for the individual to think of other matters than the maintenance of the state's existence ; and he thought of his personal existence not only in this life but in the next. He thought of it as a continuance in the next world of the life which he had led in this ; and, though he felt that his lot in the next life was dependent on his behaviour in this, he had no practical doubt that all would go well with him there. In Persia, with its dualism and in accordance with its conception of the conflict between the principles of good and evil, the same practical optimism was promoted by the reflection that Persians were all followers of Ormuzd, with whom ultimate victory in the conflict would rest, and that all other peoples were followers of Ahriman, and so doomed in the end to consuming flames. In its practical outcome the Mahommedan view differs little from the Persian.

But, whereas optimism of a sort—an optimism which leads the individual to count with confidence on Paradise for himself, and to regard with satisfaction or composure the torments reserved for those who are, from his point of view, infidels— is characteristic of the views described, the characteristic of Buddhist teaching is pessimism. In other religions the place of torment is in the next life : in Buddha's view existence itself is evil— this life it is which is Hell ; and Nirvāna is the escape from it. Nirvāna is attained by abstaining wholly from desire. It is the consummation of the prohibitive aspect of religion and morality— the negative " thou shalt not," made universal with a ruthlessness possible, perhaps, in logic, but not in life.

Buddhism directs itself to the cessation and

B

eradication of desire. In ancient Egypt and Persia, as in modern Mohammedanism, the next world was conceived as one in which the perpetual gratification of desire was to be achieved. But whether the final end is to be looked for in the total eradication of desire, or in its gratification, here and hereafter, the tacit assumption in either case is that man's desires are to be taken as the starting-point, and that the proper mode of dealing with them is the end to be aimed at. To this aim and end the gods are secondary and subsidiary. They were there primarily to assist man to escape or avoid calamity ; and later to assist man to do his will. In Christ's teaching this disposition of the universe is wholly overturned : it is no longer man that is the centre of the universe but God. Man's desires are not taken as the starting-point, nor their gratification as the end. The end to be achieved is God's will, not man's. The motive to it is love—love of God and of one's neighbour. The end is no longer the prohibitive " thou shalt not," but positive : thou shalt love thy neighbour and thy God. This life is not, as in Buddhism, of its nature hell ; but a world in which it is possible for God's kingdom to come, and His will to be done. As to the next world, the conviction that the Divine will is to be accomplished in every man, that the perfect work of love will be fulfilled, is to the Christian the

guarantee and the meaning of future life. The interpretation, however, of the next world as a place of
future punishments and rewards still commends
itself to those who cry for justice and who imagine
they have no need for a God of mercy or for forgiveness of trespasses. Nevertheless the solution of
the problem of the relation existing between man
and God which Christianity offers is that the
relation is one of love.

And the same solution is offered by Christianity
for the problem of the proper relation of man to
man. From the beginning, from the time when
man was man, there must have been in every community of human beings some trust between man
and man, if the community was to continue ; some
affection between man and woman, parent and
child. But " first principles operate long before
they come to the surface of thought and are
expounded." Love is and has been operative in
every community, otherwise it would not be a community, but it is and has been least operative in the
least developed. It is in the custom of a community
that morality first manifests itself ; but custom
sanctions at first many things, by means of taboo,
which later are dropped or are forbidden by morality.
The violation of custom and of the customary morality
of the community is interpreted and is felt to be an
offence against the being to whom the community

turns in its attempt to escape from calamity, or to avert it. Hence the fact that the will of the gods, in matters of morality, is regarded exclusively as forbidding offences and trespasses. Fear, therefore, is the emotion most operative in the early history of religion and morality. But if it is fear, it is the " fear of the Lord," which may be " the beginning of wisdom." From that fear, however—and therefore from that beginning of wisdom—escape has been sought and found in Brahminism by the development of the rite of sacrifice to a point at which it makes man master of the gods. In Greece anthropomorphism left room for fear, perhaps, but tended to make respect for the gods increasingly difficult.

CHAPTER II

SACRIFICE

In the history of religion the most important rite is that of sacrifice.

As a matter of history it has been universal ; and if the offering of animal sacrifice no longer plays any part in Buddhism, Mahommedanism, or Christianity, still it was customary and important in the religions of which they were reforms or developments, as it was in all the other religions of the world, whether their history is known to us from records and documents, or inferred by means of the Comparative Method.

Its significance for the history of religion, however, lies in the fact that by its means men everywhere have sought to establish, renew and maintain communication, and to enjoy communion, with their gods. Such communion is the essential function of religion ; and the means whereby men have sought it, and the reasons why in three great religions of the world they have abandoned the offering of animal sacrifice as a means, are of cardinal importance for the history of religion.

Wherever the rite of sacrifice is found, it is the

rite by which the community, as a community, obtains access to its Lord, and comes before his presence. The rite of private sacrifice and the use of the rite as a means by which a private individual for his private ends obtains access to the god is plainly later than the public institution. Further, as the offering of sacrifice by the community to its gods has been universal, whereas the offering of sacrifice to deceased ancestors is not universal in the historical religions of the world, we may regard sacrifice to ancestral spirits as modelled on and borrowed from sacrifice to the gods of the community. Offerings to ancestors are made only by the family descended from those ancestors: the next-door neighbours have no part in the worship. The worship is therefore not common to any two families. Still less is it a ceremonial common to all the families which together form the community. In fine, it is no part of the community's worship. It is the particular family and not the community as a whole which gathers together to worship the ancestors of that particular family.

Confining ourselves to the religions of the world other than Buddhism, Mohammedanism, and Christianity, we note that universally sacrifices are offered to the gods. Universally, too, they are offered by the community, or on its behalf, by some properly accredited official. We may, therefore, set aside the numerous cases in which offerings are made for the purpose of bringing an individual into communion or contact with the deity, as when he attaches to a sacred tree, or throws into a sacred well, something that has been, actually, or in his opinion, part of himself. The community, when it approaches its deity, so usually offers, not part of itself but some article of food, that we are bound to regard food as being the normal offering made. Where other articles than articles of food are offered, as for instance spears, shields, arrows, materials for dress, etc., are offered by the Shintoists of Japan, they are either offered by individuals, and therefore do not fall to be considered when we are concerned with the sacrifices offered by the community ; or, if offered by the community, they are less usual than offerings of food. It is better, therefore, to start by considering the offerings which are normally made by a community to its gods.

The offerings normally made are offerings of food, animal or vegetable. It is not, however, usually at the option of the worshippers to offer either animal or vegetable food as may be the more convenient for them. To each deity there are certain things which alone by custom can be offered ; and where custom has come to allow, within limits, a choice, it is possible that originally no choice was allowed. The latitude of choice may have come about because two sets of rites have coalesced into one worship. In some cases it is certain and in others highly probable that originally only one kind of offering could be made to the particular deity. To some deities animal sacrifices may not be offered ; to others no sacrifice that is bloodless may be made.

The motive with which sacrifices are offered by a community is to avert calamity from the community, or to obtain benefits for it. If, for this purpose, offerings simply, or offerings of food simply, were all that was required, then any article of food would serve to propitiate any god. But this is patently not the case : for a particular god a particular offering alone would serve. Why this should be the case is a question on which possibly light may be thrown by the fact that in some cases the deity to whom an animal or plant is offered bears the name of the plant or animal. In Mexico and in ancient Greece the deity to whom maize in the one case and corn in the other was offered bore the name of the Maize-mother or the Corn-mother—and the Corn-mother, to whom a sheaf is offered, or who is represented by a sheaf, is a figure well-known in the folk-lore of Europe. The Corn-deity is present, to the mind of her worshippers, in each and every sheaf, inasmuch as she is the corn, and each and every sheaf is corn ; and any sheaf may be preserved and reverenced as a manifestation of the Corn-deity. If preserved and reverenced, as the maize-sheaf was in Mexico, and the corn-sheaf is, as a survival, in modern Europe, the sheaf may come to be regarded from one point of view as the deity, and from another as an offering to the deity. The cakes of dough, or the figures of dough, which are made from the cereal, are also capable of wearing the same double aspect ; and, inasmuch as in Mexico the worshippers partook of the cakes, the ritual was, as the Spanish conquerors of Mexico noted with amazement, in the nature of a communion.

It is natural to seek to explain animal sacrifice in the same way as the cereal offerings in Mexico are doubtless to be explained. But there are difficulties in the way of doing so. Animal sacrifice, we may reasonably suppose, was practised long before animals were domesticated and long before cereals were cultivated. It is, therefore, unsafe to explain animal sacrifice by a principle which may not have arisen until long after animal sacrifice had established itself as an institution. The rite, again, of eating, or, participating in, the offerings made to a deity, is everywhere found in connection with animal sacrifice ; and it was probably an institution firmly established before plants were cultivated or corn-deities worshipped. Further, the mystical view of the ceremony of eating the dough figures of the deity is to be found practically only in Mexico. At any rate it cannot be considered to be anything but exceptional in the history of sacrifice : it is not the view usually entertained in the religions of the world, about the meaning and import of the sacrificial meal.

In the case of animal-worship, as of the worship of corn-deities or maize-goddesses, the god may be supposed to be equally manifest in any and every individual of the species, and limited to no one individual specimen. The name " bull " belongs equally of right to all individual members of the species ; and, in the case of a bull-deity or calf-deity, the deity may, and perhaps originally was, reverenced equally in every animal of the kind. So far there is resemblance between animal-deities and cereal-deities. And it is generally the case that in animal sacrifice it is a domesticated animal which is offered, as in the case of plant offerings it is a cultivated plant which is offered.

If, therefore, we had good grounds for supposing that all deities to whom animals are sacrificed were, or in their origin had been, animal deities, we might suppose that the animal offered to a deity bore the same double aspect, as the sheaf of maize or the dough cake or image, and was at once and mystically the offering made and the deity himself. But there are deities, such as the sky-god, the sun and moon and stars, who are not animal gods, and whose worship, for anything we can suppose, is as old as the worship of animal gods. Further, if in every case, the animal god bore the double aspect of the offering made and the deity himself, then we ought to find that in the worship of an animal god the animal was the sacrifice made. But we do not find this to be the usual case.

We have, therefore, to recognise that though to cereal deities cereal offerings were usually made, and though a similar principle may in some cases have been observed in the worship of animal deities, there are many deities in whose worship no such principle did or could apply. For a particular deity a particular offering alone would serve ; and though in some cases we can divine the reason, in the vast majority we cannot ; and, as far as we can see, the reason may well have been capricious and accidental.

Still the fact remains that the offerings generally made to the gods are offerings of food—cereals when cereals are cultivated, domestic animals where they are domesticated, and others when plants and animals are not as yet domesticated. And in view of the indispensibility of food to man, and of the uncertainty of the supply in times before the domestication of animals and plants, it seems conceivable that food, or rather edible plants and animals, may not only have been sacred, but may have been the earliest and only gods. Important, however, as food is—and man, when most of his time and energy was spent in obtaining food, must have attributed great importance to it—it is not against famine only that man has to contend : other calamities besides famine visit him ; and it is against all the misfortunes which can befall a community that the community seeks divine aid. As a general rule any one divinity can grant any request whatever that his worshippers may prefer. The principle of division of labour naturally comes later amongst the gods, than it does amongst mankind.

The more probable conclusion then seems to be that animals were sacrificed and food was generally offered, not because the gods were edible animals deified, but because the practice of making offerings arose at a period when food was difficult to obtain and was the most valuable offering that could be made, and the most acceptable offering that could be imagined.

The evidence afforded by the Comparative Method points clearly to the conclusion that originally, the being, to whom calamity was ascribed, and to whom consequently the offering was made, was simply besought to go away. The food-offering accordingly was left to be consumed by him. At a later stage, when the establishment of good relations was demonstrated by the removal of the calamity, the sacrifice or a portion of it was offered to the god, and then the community partook of the remainder. The feast was thus, from the nature of the case, a festival of rejoicing, because it marked the fact that good relations between the community and its god had been restored. In this way, eating with the god is naturally regarded as ceremonial and of high religious significance. It is felt to be the renewal of the bond between the community and its god ; and it may come to be interpreted, and by the Shintoists of Japan and the Israelites it did come to be interpreted, as pointing to a covenant made in time past between the god and his people.

In some cases, however, to this day the sacrifice of the animal to the god is not followed by a feast. In most of the historical religions of the world there are some gods of whose offerings the community does not partake. That is to say, in most religions there survives the earliest form of sacrifice —that in which the animal sacrificed is left entirely for the god. That this is a survival of the earliest form and function of sacrifice, which has for its object simply to beseech the god to go away, is indicated by the fact that it is to the gods who bring calamity and to the sinister gods of the nether world that offerings are made of which the community does not partake.

If sacrifices were originally offered only on occasions when calamity befell the community, then sacrifice was originally a rite of irregular occurrence. If they were renewed with rejoicing and thanksgiving on the removal of the calamity, such as pestilence or famine, they were still rites of irregular occurrence. Such irregularly occurring rites are yet found in the historical religions. But they are less frequent than the sacrifices which regularly recur at stated seasons. The regularly recurring rites recur annually in spring and autumn ; and though they may have come to be practised annually before plants and animals were domesticated, there is no doubt that in the historical religions they are the rites which accompany the spring festivals associated with the sowing, and the autumn festivals associated with the ingathering of the crops. The domestication of plants and the advent of cereal deities did much towards the creation of a religious calendar ; and the worship of the sun, moon and stars was that which led to the scientific calendar.

Thus far our attention has been confined to rites in which food was offered and animals were sacrificed. We cannot, however, close our eyes to the fact that human sacrifice is known, though in the historical religions it is of rare occurrence. In the religions which have no recorded history it is also found and we may probably regard it as an institution of great antiquity, even though normally of irregular occurrence.

The explanation of disaster which befalls a community is found in the assumption, which to early man seems self-evident, that it is the doing of some being or person. The being or person, therefore, must have been offended by the community, and can only have been so offended because some member of the community has done what he should not have done. The ultimate cause of the calamity, therefore, on this showing, is a departure, on the part of some person or other, from the custom of the tribe, and a violation of taboo. If the offender can be detected, he is punished by being excluded from the community, temporarily or permanently, as being tabooed ; or if the calamity from which the community is suffering be great, he may be executed. Such execution was regarded by the Gauls, for instance, as being "a purification of society for the purpose of re-establishing more harmonious relations with a deity." As the offender was executed and good relations with the deity restored, it was easy to regard the offender as having been offered as a sacrifice to the deity, and as having been accepted as such.

When once the feeling has established itself that

in time of great calamity, the deity, being wroth with the community, demands the death of some member of the community, then the sacrifice of any member is regarded as sufficing to appease the offended deity ; and—as in the case of the Gauls—the execution or sacrifice of an innocent member will be as potent as that of a criminal. Then, for a member of the community, a war-captive may be substituted ; or, if captives be not forthcoming, a voluntary victim may be obtained. At Marseilles, as elsewhere, when the inhabitants were suffering from a pestilence, a pauper was induced, by the prospect of being maintained for a year in luxury at the expense of the community, to offer himself, and so to purify the whole community.

Thus the offering of human victims, as being a means to avert calamity from the community, goes back to the earliest purpose and function of sacrifice, though it cannot be regarded as the earliest form assumed by the rite. It is most common in religions which have no recorded history ; and disappears as a rule from the historical religions, or leaves but occasional traces.

That is the normal history of the rite of human sacrifice, as revealed by a comparison of religions ; but the Comparative Method, for the very reason that it dwells on the resemblances between the various religions of the world, calls attention to the points of unlikeness. One state there has been which attained to a considerable degree of civilisation, and which, instead of allowing human sacrifice to dwindle into a mere survival, or to disappear altogether, developed it to a monstrous and almost incredible extent. Amongst the Aztecs of Mexico, not only for the purpose of averting famines, such as that which commenced in 1445 and lasted for several years, were numerous human sacrifices offered to the gods, but the brilliant success with which their empire grew was ascribed to the human sacrifices, by means of which the favour of the gods was regularly purchased. "Every festival, every victory, the commencement of every cycle of years, every accession to the throne, every dedication of a temple, was celebrated with blood-stained offerings, and the more important the festival, the more numerous were the sacrifices."

In Mexico, as in Marseilles and elsewhere, some of the victims were for a year maintained in luxury. What comes out plainly in the Mexican instance is that, for the year, the victim was regarded as an incarnation of the god to whom he was eventually to be sacrificed. This fact, evidently, must be taken in connection with the mystical view of the ritual which in Mexico was associated with the worship of cereal deities. In that worship the sheaf, or the dough, may be regarded either as the

c

deity or as the offering to the deity. The deity was conceived in human form, and the dough or paste was made into figures of human form, of which the worshippers partook, as, before the domestication of plants, they had partaken of the animal sacrifices offered to the gods. Hence the mystical view that, in partaking of the paste figures, the worshippers were not merely sharing in an offering that had been made to the god, or eating with him, but that they were in actual fact eating the god. Human sacrifice is found where domesticated plants are unknown ; and it may well have existed amongst the Aztecs before the cult of the maize-mother or other cereal deities. By contamination the cult of the cereal deities, and that of the gods to whom human sacrifice was offered, would soon affect each other. The dough figures would be regarded as less potent offerings than human victims ; and human victims would come to be regarded as not merely offerings to the deity, but as being identical with the god, in the same mystic manner in which the sheaf, or the dough figure of the deity, was the actual embodiment of the god.

In the Aztecs we have a warrior-nation who offered their war-captives to the gods, as did the Babylonians, Assyrians, and ancient Egyptians. But, as would be evident from the overgrowth of ritual, if we had no other evidence, priesthood had

developed amongst the Aztecs of the fifteenth
century at least as much as it had amongst their
Spanish conquerors of the same date, though the
cruelties of the Inquisition did not equal the excesses
promoted by the Aztec priests.

For another instance of the abnormal development of which the rite of sacrifice is capable in the
hands of a priesthood, we must turn to the Vedic,
or Brahmin, religion. Here, however, the excess is
offensive to the reason and religious feeling rather
than revolting to the senses : the smell of human
blood is no longer in the air.

In the Vedic religion, as in all other religions,
sacrifice was originally a meal offered to the gods.
The form of sacrifice which possesses the most
primitive character, and appears to be the oldest,
is that of the " south fire " (dâkshinâgni), which
has for its object to induce the beings, to whom it
is offered, simply to go away. And even the great
horse-sacrifice, which is " the King of Sacrifice,"
the culminating point of the ancient cult, and a
sacrifice in which the whole community takes its
part, is still a sacrifice undertaken for the protection
of the community. The annually recurring festivals
of sacrifice, in this as in other religions, are those
which are associated with agricultural operations.
In addition, however, to the festivals, which occur
elsewhere, at the time of sowing and of harvest,

there is one which naturally grew up in a land which is so dependent on rain, and in which the breaking of the monsoons is so all-important, and that is the sacrifice for rain.

In the Vedic religion, as in others, the " nature-gods " are intimately bound up with the elements, or nature-powers, through which they manifest themselves. The same word, *agni*, designates both " fire " and the " fire-god." Indra, the god of lightning, is also the lightning itself. The same word, *dyâus*, stands both for the sky and the sky-god ; though the god is also known as *dyâus pitar*, " father-sky," as in Mexico the same word, *Xilonen*, stands both for " young ear of maize " and the goddess of maize, while in Peru the goddess was known as *Sara-mama*, " mother-maize."

Whereas in other religions food-offerings are more important than drink-offerings, in the Vedic religion period libations were at least of equal importance. And that the importance of drink-offerings goes back to a time when the Aryan invaders of India had not yet separated from their kinsmen who invaded Persia, is shown both by the etymological identity of the words used—*soma* and *haoma*—and by the importance which attached to libations in the religions of both peoples.

The resemblances, then, which the Comparative Method reveals between the religion of the Aryan invaders of India and that of other peoples in the same stage of evolution, are manifest. But it is the differences, disclosed by the Comparative Method, which are of interest to us now.

The differences may be summed up in the one word Brahminism. The Bráhman who offers prayer gets his name from the prayer, brahmán, which he offers. Brahminism is a religious system which is centred in prayer, which, we may say without exaggeration, exists for prayer, and begins and ends in prayer. The god who attained to supremacy over all the other gods provided by the Vedas was Brahma ; and Brahma is simply prayer. It is prayer, however, for escape from calamity or for the bestowal of external goods. It is not the prayer of thanksgiving : the word for " thanks " is not to be found in the vocabulary of the Vedas.

In the same way that the prayer offered to the gods eventually became a god, so the libation—soma—offered to the gods became a god, Soma.

Thus we see that the sacrifice—the libation or prayer which originally was a means for approaching the gods and attaining the ends desired by man —came, in Brahminism, to be no longer the means but the end itself. The ritual of libation and sacrifice, at first performed reverently, became itself an object of reverence, the supreme object of reverence. As at an earlier stage in the history of this religion the same word meant both " fire " and " fire-god," or " sky " and " sky-god," so now the word for " prayer " came to mean the " prayer-god," and the rite became itself the supreme god, Brahma, whose ministers the Brahmins are.

It is obvious that this development is one which could not have taken place, had not circumstances favoured the development of a caste of priests. And it is precisely in India that the caste system has been evolved and is carried to the extreme. The word for caste is *varna*, and means " colour." It points to a distinction of colour between the invading Aryans and the aboriginal population that they conquered. When once it had come to be used as a term of distinction between the conquerors and the conquered population of Çudras, reduced to the position of hewers of wood and drawers of water, it would easily come to be applied to the differences of occupation amongst the conquerors themselves, to distinguish the artisans, the Vaiçyas, from the ruling classes ; and it would be equally applicable to distinguish the priestly caste of the Brahmins from the warrior caste of Kshatriyas.

When the ritual of prayer and sacrifice or libation has become, as in the hands of a priesthood it tends to become, an end in itself, the god comes to be a negligible quantity, or, at the best, to be at the disposal of the priest. This attitude of the priest to the god is stated quite frankly in the Vedas : " The priest who celebrates the sacrifice pursues Indra, as a hunter his prey : he seizes on him as a bird-catcher seizes the bird ; the god is a wheel which he knows how to turn." The gods are conceived as attending on the sacrifice, for it is from the libation and sacrifice they derive their strength : " as the ox bellows for rain, so yearns Indra for the soma."

Thus, in the outcome, as the Brahmin lived only to perform the sacrificial rite, he taught that the rite of sacrifice was the originating cause and the final end of the existence of the gods. " The world was created by the sacrificial rite : from the sacrificial rite the gods are sprung." Sacrifice had its origin in heaven ; and the heavenly sacrifice is the prototype of all earthly sacrifices. In Brahminism sacrifice is the beginning and the end of all things. And the sacrifice is performed by the Brahmins.

In no other religion of the world has ritual, the means of bringing the community into the presence of the Lord, come so effectually to substitute itself for the end desired by the community, as it has in Brahminism. Amongst the Persians, who are nearest akin to the Aryan invaders of India, and who closely resemble them in many points of their religion—for instance, in their view of soma (haoma) and their worship of fire—sacrifice is regarded, as it was in the Vedic religion, as the rite whereby not only man gains divine help, but the gods themselves derive strength. But in Persia the world-process was regarded as a struggle between the powers of good and evil, Ormuzd and Ahriman ; and consequently the sacrificial rite never became an end in itself ; it remained always a means by which man, for his part, assisted the gods in their fight.

In Assyria and Babylonia the sacrificial rite was not indeed viewed as having created the world : the priests were content to teach merely that it had existed from the time of the creation. Sacrifice was the daily meal enjoyed twice a day by the gods. But though the gods are represented in Babylonia, with a simile almost as forcible as any in the Vedas, to " swarm round the sacrifice like flies," they never, as in Brahminism, became negligible quantities. In a military despotism and a despotic empire, such as this, sacrifice was regarded as a tribute paid by man to the gods.

From ancient Egypt we have less information about the ritual of sacrifice, and we may infer safely that its development was carried to no exaggerated degree. The fate of the soul in the next world was a matter of much more personal interest to the individual. In China sacrifice was made to the gods in the same way, for the same reasons and at the same seasons, as it was offered elsewhere to the gods. But ancestor-worship developed to such an extent in China as effectually prevented any exaggerated importance being attributed to the ritual followed in sacrifices to the gods.

In Israel, as elsewhere, there were two classes of sacrifice : those which were intended to avert calamity and atone for the offences which provoked it, and those which were feasts, partaken of first by the deity, and then by the community of worshippers. In Israel the forces which elsewhere checked the development of the rite of sacrifice were wanting. Ancestor-worship, which flourished in China as an effectual counterpoise, either had as little attraction for the Israelites as it had for the Assyrians and Babylonians, or, if it had more, it found in Jehovah a jealous god, whose ministers suffered it not to grow. The continuation of this life in the next world, which absorbed much of the Egyptian's thought, and diverted much of his attention from the ritual of sacrifice, was a matter on which the Israelites, again like the Assyrians and Babylonians, did not speculate. It was on this life that the interests of the Israelites were concentrated ; but, whereas in Assyria recourse was had to magic to avert the calamities which befall man, in Israel the worship of Jehovah was early established on so strong a footing in the consciousness of the community, that magic never succeeded in attaining to noticeable growth.

In these circumstances the ritual of sacrifice might have been expected to develop in Israel, if not in the same way, then, though in some other way, to as great an extent as it did in other religions, which provided no counter-poise to it. But in Israel its development was stayed in a way peculiar to Israel and of great importance in the history of religion. The arrest of its development was the work of the Hebrew prophets, beginning with Jeremiah and Ezekiel. They taught that the Lord took no delight in the blood of sheep and rams ; that He would have obedience, not sacrifice. The importance of their work lies in the fact that, whereas down to their time worship had been an affair of the community, they taught that worship, to be religious, must be personal communion with God. According to the inherited view, it was the community alone which could appear before the Lord, and with sacrifice, and by means of sacrifice alone, that it could so appear. The ritual of sacrifice, the rites by means of which alone the community could obtain access to the Lord, were in the hands of the priests. It was for the priests, therefore, to maintain the traditional, which was indeed the national, conception, that religion was the rela-tion, maintained and renewed by the offering of sacrifices, between Jehovah and His people, the Jewish nation.

This conception, according to which the Jews regarded themselves as the chosen nation, chosen of the Lord, and the rest of the world as heathen, is the same as that which led the Persians to regard themselves as followers of Ormuzd, and to consider the rest of mankind to be marked off for destruction as followers of Ahriman. In the beginning indeed, in all cases, the political community and the religious community are co-extensive and identical ; and, for long after, the disruption of either is taken to involve the disruption of the other. The worship of the Babylonian pantheon, for instance, lasted no longer than the Babylonian empire. It is on the priests, therefore, who, by maintaining the national worship, maintain the relations between the nation and the nation's gods, that the duty falls of up-holding the national worship of which they are the ministers.

In Israel the official and priestly view of sacrifice was the view which was traditional and usual in the religion of other nations. It was that by the sacrificial ritual relations were maintained not between individual members of the community and the god, but between the community and him. This view excludes the conception of personal communion ; if strictly and successfully maintained, it prevents the growth of personal religion, and, in any event, blights it.

It was against this view that the Hebrew prophets preached, and it was the success of their teaching that made personal religion possible. The Jewish people, however, is tenacious of the old ways, more tenacious indeed than any other nation, as may be illustrated from the fact that it still retains two bequests from pre-historic times which have been declined by other civilised peoples—the practice of circumcision and the taboo on an article of food. It is, therefore, in perfect consistency with this national characteristic of tenacity that they have retained the ritual of animal sacrifice. The prophetic movement, therefore, away from sacrifice, was one which, as events showed, could not reach its culmination within the Jewish community, but, to be carried out, had to be transplanted into the wider community of mankind.

Thus, in two religions, the Jewish and the Brahmin, the ritual of sacrifice was developed, on different lines, to a greater extent than in any other religion in the world. In both it led to a movement which was a reaction, in the sense that it abolished the rite of sacrifice as the means or the condition of religious life, but was a forward movement, in the sense that it disengaged two of the most potent religions in the world—Christianity and Buddhism.

Each of these eventually had to abandon its home of origin, Judæa and India, so firmly was the ritual of sacrifice embedded there. Both became missionary religions, and were assisted in becoming so by the fact that they had abandoned the conception, up to that point universal in all religions, that a religious community to exist at all must be a State-community. Both were destined to demonstrate by their life and action that only by ceasing to be dependent on a political community can a religion have the chance of becoming the religion of mankind —though Christianity may more correctly be said to be demonstrating this truth than to have become fully conscious of it, save in the mission-field.

Formally, and in words, indeed, it may be disputed whether Buddhism, which is a reaction against the ritual of sacrifice, as the condition whereby a community is brought before its Lord, and the means of religious life, is, or can be, a personal religion. But in actual fact it is persons to whom it appeals, and persons amongst whom it spreads. Formally, and in words again, it may be disputed whether Buddhism, which in its theory finds no place for any god, can be a religion at all. But in actual fact, Buddha is worshipped as a god.

Whatever the inconsistencies in Buddhism, the fact remains that it was born in reaction against Brahminism and its exaggerated development of the sacrificial rite. It is a community not political, entrance into which is determined not by birth but by conversion of the individual—the personal resolution henceforth to turn to the truth which Buddha taught.

In Brahminism and Judaism we have seen the ritual of sacrifice and the importance of the rite pushed to a point of exaggeration which provoked reaction, and which, in Judæa at least, stimulated the growth of personal religion. In ancient Greece the rite was not merely incompatible with personal religion—for in Greece as elsewhere those who appeared at the community's sacrifices did so collectively and not as individual persons—it became an active force in undermining personal religion.

The dependence of man on his God for delivery from evil and for his daily bread is implicit in the idea of sacrifice from the beginning, for from the beginning the god is conceived as the being who can remove calamity and who can bestow material blessings. The relation between the community and its god is capable of being conceived and interpreted—as it is both in the Shintoism of Japan and amongst the Israelites—as resting on a covenant between them whereby he is to be their god and they are to be his people. And the covenant may further be conceived as having been originated by the god, as it was conceived to have been by the

Israelites. Such a conception originates in some highly religious mind, and testifies to a highly religious view of the world.

But though the sacrificial rite is capable of presenting itself in this light to those who practise it, it is also capable of other interpretations. So long as the parties to the rite are the god on the one hand and the community on the other, so long as the people appear before their Lord bearing gifts, the gifts are understood as expressing the community's sense of its dependence on the god. They are offerings to the Lord, or, as in Assyria and Babylon, a tribute paid to Him as to a king ; and, the more solemn and elaborate the ceremonial becomes, the greater becomes the distance between those who make the offerings or pay the tribute, and the god who receives them. Thus, as the community, which is one of the parties to the rite, develops from a tribe into an imperial state, the might and majesty of the gods, who are the other party to the rite, tends to increase in the same ratio. The sacrifice is conceived as an offering to the Lord which is made of bounden duty ; and is not susceptible of being misinterpreted as a gift, or present, or bribe. At the same time, the sacrifice is made by the community for the public good, and not for the benefit of any private individual.

When, however, as eventually comes to be the

case (except where an organised priesthood, as in Israel, prevents it) private individuals succeed in inducing the ministers of the rite to allow them to offer sacrifice for their private ends, the rite of sacrifice becomes an active force in undermining personal religion.   In Greece it came to be a means of gratifying personal desire and of securing that man's will be done.   The relation which private sacrifice established between man and the gods he prayed to became one in which the individual's thoughts were fixed on what he was to gain by the transaction, and in which the god tended to become the other party to the bargain. Not only were the gods anthropomorphised in outward semblance, but the divine personality was lowered from that of a king and disposer supreme to that of a seller of goods in the market-place.

Thus, in Greece, the attempt made to establish a personal relation between the individual and his God, and to advance from the religion of the community to personal religion, resulted in the still further degradation of the anthropomorphic gods. The ritual of sacrifice, so long as the community alone was admitted to it, excluded the individual: when it admitted him, and by admitting him, it manifested itself as a means of gratifying his desires, not his aspirations.

CHAPTER III

MAGIC

AGAINST the calamities and misfortunes which may
befall the community it is conceived to be the
business of the community to provide, by appeals
to the powers worshipped by the community.
Where, as in Japan and in Israel, the relation of
man to the gods was conceived to be in the nature of
a covenant between them, it was the community
that was a party to the covenant, and not any
individual member of the community; and the
contractual obligation of the gods bound them to
avert calamity from the community, but not to
protect any particular person from misfortune that
affected him alone.

Against personal misfortune, such as illness or
death, it was the business of the individual to guard
himself. When, as in the earlier stages of human
evolution, everything that called for explanation
was explained by regarding it as having been done
by somebody, the illness or death of a person was
regarded as having been brought about by somebody.
The author of the calamity, therefore, was a person
actuated by malignity and having the power to

D

cause illness or death. In looking for the author
of the calamity, then, it was necessary to look for
some one who was the sort of person who would be
expected to be guilty of that sort of thing. Some
such person is always to be found by those who
expect to find him ; and he is some one who is
marked out by a strangeness of person or a forbidding
manner or an evil eye, which creates the expecta-
tion of strange or malevolent actions on his part.
He or she is believed to possess strange powers,
that is to say, is regarded as a magician or witch ;
and on him lights suspicion, when the illness or
death of a person sets those near to the sufferer
wondering who has brought the calamity about.
The suspected person may feel a certain satisfaction
in being credited with strange power and in being
approached with fear and trembling. He may be
ready to allow it to be supposed that he has strange
power : he may come eventually to be convinced
that those who ascribe it to him must be right. He
may have considerable confidence that he is a remarkable person, especially if he is conscious of
considerable will-power, or is apt to pass into states
of ecstasy or trance. And when he has come, by
whatever way, to acquiesce in the opinion which
those around him hold about him, all that he has to
do is to exercise the power which he and they feel
that he possesses. All that he can do is to express

himself in words of power with appropriate gestures. And that is all he need do, for, in the opinion of everybody, he has but to speak the word and the thing is done. He makes the gesture of dealing a blow, and the blow is dealt : it is felt by the victim however far away—and this is magic. To make sure—if his self-confidence is not quite absolute and perfect—that his blow gets home, he may make a drawing in the sand, or a figure in clay or wax, which stands for his victim, and then, as he stabs the figure, so will his victim feel the pang. This proceeding may be described in one sense of the words as a substitution of similars, but the phrase is misleading, if it leads us to forget that the actual blow which the sorcerer deals is believed to be the actual blow which the victim feels. Without this belief to start with, there would be no belief in magic. But the belief in magic is, or has been, universal ; and everywhere it is fundamentally the same, and strikingly similar in the forms which it assumes. It is not necessary here to illustrate this ; and we must return to the question of the relation of magic to religion.

In the historical religions of the world we may say generally that there is no confusion, or tendency to confusion, between magic and religion. The community's worship of its gods is an institution which is quite distinct from the individual's employment of magic, or of a magician, for his personal ends and private purposes. The distinction indeed is not merely one which is intellectually drawn : it is one which is practically felt. The difference is felt both by the person who employs magic, and by those on whom it is employed. It is liable to be employed for purposes in aid of which the assistance of the community's gods cannot be prayed, for the very good reason that those purposes are anti-social and are felt by the community to be injurious to it. When magic is employed, as it commonly was employed, to bring about the sickness or death of a member of the community, it is naturally visited by the community with condemnation ; and witch-finders may be set to work to smell out the magician, with a view to his execution. It is true that not all magic is " black magic " of this kind. The personal desires and private purposes, for the fulfilment of which magic may be set to work, are not, or are not obviously, all anti-social or injurious. Love philtres are common or universal in occurrence and are not conceived where practised to be condemnable.

Since magic is used for the private ends of the individual, it is not surprising that in ancient Egypt, where one of the most important purposes, if not the most important purpose, for which the individual had to make provision, was the next life, magical means were employed to provide the dead man with all that he might require for his continued existence. It is true that in ancient Egypt the teaching of religion was that, after death, the spirit of the deceased was brought to judgment before a tribunal of the gods. But it is also true, and even more important, that there is not, in the whole of the Book of the Dead, one single word to indicate the likelihood of condemnation; on the contrary, it is manifestly felt to be self-evident that the deceased will be acquitted. For his acquittal foresight was taken; he was provided with amulets and magical formulæ. For his welfare in the next world provision was made by the magical pictures on the walls of his tomb, which ensured that he should in the next life continue the agreeable occupations which had engaged him in this world. In this matter, therefore, in Egypt, the practice of magic was not realised to be in conflict either with morality or religion, though in fact it plainly led the Egyptian to feel that his fate in the next world was not determined according as his conduct was or was not guided by the dictates of religion and morality, but by the amulets and magical formulæ with which he was armed to meet what would befall him in the next world. It is only where magic is felt to be in conflict with the interests of the community that it is realised to be hostile to the gods whom the community worshipped, and on whose aid it relied.

In ancient Egypt, then, the incompatibility of magic and religion had not revealed itself. In Babylon the incompatibility had come to be felt and to be pronounced, presumably because the religious sentiment was stronger there than in Egypt. But magic was as deeply rooted in Babylon as in Egypt ; and, if the religious sentiment was stronger in Babylon, it was only strong enough to compromise with magic, not to eject it. It was not till Assyrian times that it gathered strength enough to cast it aside.

The compromise effected in Babylon between magic and religion is singularly interesting. It is based upon the fact that—quite apart from religion and the gods—magic can be met by counter-magic : the magician may be defeated by the exorcist. The business of the exorcist is to find out a counter-charm. The means of exorcism in Babylon were principally water, which cleanses the victim and washes away the effects of magic ; and fire, which purges and consumes it, as all other impurities and defilements. A brazier is placed by the bedside of the sick man, the exorcist murmurs words of power, and commits to the flames various substances, that the charm may be consumed and destroyed as they are, and may pass into flames as they do. The sufferer is girt with a girdle, in order that as it is unloosed so may he be freed from the sickness which

the magician has brought upon him. Images
made of clay, meal, wax or wood to represent the
magician or the witch, are laid on the head or the
feet of the sick man, and then destroyed, burnt,
cast in the river or buried under a door-sill or in the
place where the dead are interred. In all this there
is nothing to distinguish Babylonian magic or
counter-magic from magic as practised elsewhere ;
every one of the devices used in Babylonian magic
may be paralleled from the magic of other times
and places.

Exorcisms of the kind illustrated in the last
paragraph form by far the larger part of the sacred
literature of Babylon preserved to us in cuneiform.
What distinguishes them from the ordinary spells
in world-wide use is that they have prefixed to
them formulæ which intimate that their effectiveness is due to the power of the gods who are men-
tioned in the formulæ. This indicates clearly that
the spells were originally in current use, outside the
religious system, and that, when they were taken up
into the religious system, they were so incorporated
by the simple device of labelling them with a preface
which showed that they were approved and adopted
by the State religion. The approval and adoption,
however, was not merely formal. Doubtless it
means that counter-magic, being used to protect
members of the community, was felt to be very

different from the magic which was anti-social, and which existed only to injure them. Counter-magic, being thus used in the interests of the community, was something of which the gods, who were the guardians of the State, could approve; but religious sentiment demanded that it should be understood to derive its effectiveness from the gods. Hence the formulæ prefixed. Action and reaction, however, are equal. If counter-magic was thus lifted to a higher moral level than that of magic, religion was correspondingly and proportionately debased. The gods themselves, in this connection and from this point of view, were degraded to the level of magicians. The prefixing of the religious exordium could not and did not remain a mere form. The result it brought about was that the most important practical function of the most important Babylonian god, Marduk, came to be the frustration of magic. Marduk, however, was not the only god affected. As counter-magic was represented as deriving its power from Marduk, so Marduk was conceived as deriving his power of counter-magic from his father, Ea, the knower of all things, the lord of all secrets, who thus becomes a supreme counter-magician, from whom nothing is concealed, and who therefore can rend the veil of secrecy in which the malevolent worker of magic always conceals himself from his victims. As

Marduk, the morning sun that rises from the ocean,
brings the water of purification which is to wash
away the workings of malevolent magic, so the fire-
god, Girru, is implored to consume them in his
sacred fire.   And Girru is represented in the formulæ
as appealing for the power to counteract magic,
in the same way as Marduk appeals to Ea.

Thus far we have been concerned solely with
the means by which magicians, wizards and witches
were defeated in Babylon.   But their magical
power is not the only magical power against which
the Babylonian conceived it necessary to defend
himself.   In the exorcisms used for the frustration
of magic there is constant mention of the Seven
Evil Spirits.   In them are personified all sickness
and calamity : they are the forces of destruction,
the source of all the ills that befall mankind.   They
are the powers of the storm and, like the storm,
they burst upon man and beast.   They are children
of hell ; they are neither male nor female ; their
abode is in the waste places of the earth ; they
bring in their train eclipses, floods, sickness and
death.   They ride the storm on the wings of all
the four winds.

If we apply the Comparative Method to the
elucidation of these Seven Evil Spirits, it is obvious
that they are storm-spirits, such as are found all
over the world, in Teutonic mythology and in the

Shintoism of Japan alike. As a general rule, the spirits of the storm find a place amongst the deities of polytheism. In China they receive worship as the Thien-Schen. In the Shintoism of Japan they were represented as having become gods of the community in consequence of a vision that appeared to the Emperor. In the Vedas the storm-gods, Maruts, appear as a troop of wild gods of the wind in the train of Indra. The Boreas of the Greeks and the Valkyries of the Teutons come as further examples of storm-spirits worshipped as gods. If, then, the spirits of the storm elsewhere are conceived as gods and receive divine worship, the question naturally arises why, in Babylonia, they received exceptional treatment and were relegated to the position of evil spirits. If the treatment accorded to them were absolutely without parallel we might be at a loss for an explanation. But, as we shall see when we come to consider the religion of ancient Persia and the religious revolution brought about by Zarathustra, it is a fact, by no means unfamiliar in the history of religions, that the deities of an old religion come to be relegated to the category of evil spirits by a new religion which triumphs over the old. The *devas*, who, as their name indicates, were originally deities in the eyes of the common ancestors of the Persians and the Aryan Hindus, came to be *daêvas* in the sense of evil spirits in the teaching of Zarathustra. The presumption therefore afforded by the Comparative Method is that the exceptional treatment afforded to the spirits of the wind and the storm in Babylonia is to be explained in the same way as that received in Persia by the *devas*. The State system of religion in Babylonia found no place in its pantheon for the storm-spirits who had been worshipped as deities, but excluded them as evil spirits that brought pestilence and death. Against the sickness and death, therefore, brought by them, the same protection was sought as had been employed against the misfortunes caused by magicians. Counter-magic was set to work to counteract sickness and disease whether brought about by magicians or by evil spirits. And to counteract the maleficence of these evil spirits was specially incumbent on the State gods who had refused them admission to the pantheon. Thus there was another practical reason for incorporating into the State religion the counter-magic by which it was the custom of the people to counteract sickness, and seek to avert death. And the result of this incorporation was that, whereas magic originally was conceived to be always the doing of some human being, now it came to be regarded as the way in which evil spirits also acted. Consequently, whereas counter-magic had been sufficient to meet the magic employed by witches and warlocks, to meet the magical powers of the Seven Evil Spirits there was required not only exorcism but the power of the gods which is invoked in the formulæ prefixed to Babylonian exorcisms.

But though religious sentiment in Babylonia for a time tolerated this invasion of the religious domain by magic, eventually in the Assyrian period a reaction came. Sickness and calamity may be regarded as the work of evil beings, such as the Seven Evil Spirits, or of one evil being, such as the Ahriman of the ancient Persian dualistic system. But they may also be interpreted as solely due to the wrath of a deity justly offended. This is implicit in the early conception of the relation of the community to its god. The misfortune which befalls a community is interpreted as due to some offence against the god, committed by some member of the community. This view of the relation of men to their gods is the view which reasserts itself in the Assyrian Penitential Psalms. The conviction which underlies them and finds expression throughout them is that the guardian deity of the offending individual must be approached with lamentation and penitence, not that the magician or demon must be defeated by means of counter-magic. But here the early view of the relation of men to their gods has undergone an important modification, or has evolved in a significant manner. On the early view it was calamity to the community which revealed that some offence against the community's god must have been committed. But the attitude of the penitent in the Assyrian Penitential Psalms is that misfortune, befalling him individually, has revealed to him that he personally has committed some transgression. And it is not to the gods of the community, who have at least the community's interests at heart, though they care for no one beyond the community, that the penitent goes, but to his particular guardian deity.

CHAPTER IV

In the historical religions of the world the idea that human personality continues after the death of the body, whether the conception was an inference drawn from premises or one realised as an inde-feasible aspect of personality itself, is an idea present in all of them.

The human person who acts and does things comes to be identified with the " double " of the living, or the " ghost " of the dead, man, which appears in dreams. Thus it is the continuance of other people, rather than of oneself, after death that is first recognised. That is to say, it was the objective side of personality that was first recognised, as it still is in the history of every child ; persons are to the child, at first, objects of thought or apprehension. Indeed, it is the objective side even of himself that the child first realises : it takes him some time before he can use the personal pronoun " I " in the nominative case, and can realise that in himself, or of himself, there is not only the objective aspect of personality which presents itself to others, but something subjective also.

The first thing recognised is, as has just been said, the continuance of other people after death ; that is to say, it is the continuance of the objective aspect, the double of the living man, or the ghost of the dead one, which is first assumed and speculated on. And, in the objective aspect which other people present to us, the body plays an important part. So important is its part that in ancient Egypt the continuance of the soul after death was conceived to depend on the preservation of the body ; and in Christianity the resurrection of the body is in some sense a condition of life after death. From this point of view the subjective side of personality is not only indefeasibly connected with its objective side, just as a line must have two sides to be a line, but the objective side—that which we most readily realise in other people—is identified with the body, on the hasty assumption that in other people the only reality is the body, and that in their case the line has not two sides, but only one.

In other, and in most of the other historical religions, however, the question, what are the fortunes of a person after his body is dead, was felt to be much less practical and much less interesting to the survivors than the question, how to deal with the ghost that was apt to revisit and disturb the survivors. The practical question was how to induce the ghost to go away and to stay away ;

and funeral rites and ceremonies are generally, and may well originally have always been, designed and maintained simply to keep the ghost away. The dead are the departed : they have gone away. They return, as ghosts, only exceptionally ; and then because they have not been buried, or have not been buried properly. The appearance of the dead in dreams, or as ghosts, in itself a disquieting appearance, is interpreted, when once funeral rites have become customary, as indicating that the body has not been properly and effectually disposed of ; and thus a reason to account for the return of the dead man is found in the anger which he is supposed to feel at not having received the obsequies which are due to the dead.

As at the present day some persons believe in ghosts or visits from the dead, and others do not, so some of the historical religions of the world have found accommodation for the belief, while others, for instance the Babylonian, Assyrian and Jewish, have taught definitely that from the other world the dead do not return ; and, of course, in a religion in which souls are believed to transmigrate from body to body, they cannot, consistently, appear as ghosts.

In those religions which taught that travellers to the other world do not return, there is no opportunity for ancestor-worship ; and, where ancestor-worship occurs, speculation as to the future state is answered before it can begin—the only aspect of the dead which interests the living is their activity in the affairs of this world. The early Greeks and Romans, like the Chinese of the present day, were more interested in the way in which they themselves might be affected by the spirits of their dead than they were in the fortunes of the departed, or the nature of their abode.

In all three of these countries, however, the practice was to place in the grave, with the corpse, all the things of which he might have need ; and the object with which this was done was evidently that the dead might have no reason for returning. What was desired was that he would go away, and stay away. A way of effecting this, which may even be older than the practice of burying the dead, is one which is found amongst some uncivilised tribes, and is found as a survival in China. Amongst the former it consists in simply abandoning the dwelling of the dead man and everything that belonged to him. In China the whole house in which the death took place is now, formally and ceremonially, abandoned ; in earlier days it was actually abandoned for a time ; and originally it may have been abandoned altogether.

Whether, then, the dead man's house and property were deserted, or whether his property was buried,

E

or burnt, along with his body, the object of the proceeding was to deprive the deceased of any excuse for returning. Thus the things abandoned in this way came to be regarded, naturally, as offerings made to the deceased. At first they were made on the occasion of the funeral to induce him to go away. Then they came to be repeated, after an interval, to ensure his staying away ; in China the family grave is visited, and offerings are made in April and at the winter-solstice ; in Rome the similar ceremonies were celebrated at the Parentalia, in February, and at the Larentalia, in December ; in Greece the annual offerings were made in February.

Thus far the only purpose with which the offerings were made was to induce the ghosts to go away and keep away ; and that, as we have seen, was probably the purpose with which originally sacrifice and offerings were made to those powers who came eventually to be worshipped as gods, and who were at first regarded as the authors simply of any calamity that befel the community. There is, therefore, a resemblance between gods and ancestral spirits. But there is also an all-important difference. It is that the persons, who had to fear calamity and provide against it, were in the one case the whole community, and in the other only the family of the deceased man. This difference is one which, from the beginning to the end, marked off ancestor-worship from the worship of the gods in an unmistakable manner : the set of worshippers, of those who had the right, and the duty, to join in the ceremonial and benefit by it, in the one case consisted of the community, and in the other simply of the family of this or that deceased man.

This all-important difference we must bear in mind, if we wish to understand how it is that in only one of the religions of the world—that of China—has ancestor-worship come to rival the worship of the gods. In all other of the great religious systems the worship of the gods has killed out ancestor-worship sooner or later, mostly sooner, and one reason for this is clear—the worship of the gods is common to all members of the community, whereas the ancestor-worship of each household is confined to that particular household. When once the community has grown into the custom of expecting the powers, whom it approaches, not only to avert calamity, but to confer positive blessings, then the gods of the community are the beings from whom the community expects blessings. From the ancestors of any particular family that family may come to expect benefits—though probably this does not come about until after the community has come to expect positive benefits from the beings that it worships.

In the historical religions it was the gods who came to be regarded as the sole source of earthly blessings. In Greece ancestor-worship died out early, and even in Rome it remained a purely private worship. In China, however, it attained, and still retains, an importance which is unique in the history of religions.

The importance, however, of ancestor-worship in China must not be supposed to be greater than that of the worship of the gods. The temples of the gods in China are to be counted by the thousand, their images by the tens of thousands. The religious life of the people has its centre in the temples of the gods. To the temples of those gods who are especially esteemed countless persons of both sexes and all ages daily flock to pray for benefits to come, and to promise sacrifice and offerings in return for them, when bestowed. There are, in China as elsewhere, gods of the clouds, winds, rain, thunder, etc. ; there are sacrifices to vegetation-deities, and annual sacrifices for rain and for harvest. Heaven—Thien—and earth, sun, and moon, the stars, rivers, and fire are worshipped in the Chinese religion as in others. The gods in China, as elsewhere, are anthropomorphic, and in their own temples are depicted in human form.

In all these points the Chinese religion resembles the other historic religions so widely and so closely that we may safely infer that in China the worship of the gods had in its origin as little to do with ancestor-worship as it had in Assyria and Babylonia, where ancestor-worship never developed. What is peculiar to China is the extent to which ancestor-worship has developed and to which it has, if not encroached on the worship of the gods, at any rate come to rank almost side by side with it. The process by which this result has been brought about has been one of levelling down and levelling up. The worship of the gods has been levelled down by causes not having anything to do with ancestor-worship ; in China, as elsewhere, sacrifice to the gods was originally offered on behalf of the community, and sacrifice to Heaven is still offered, on behalf of the community, by the Emperor, or was so offered before the institution of the Chinese Republic. But, as elsewhere, so in China, private individuals have come to offer to the gods private sacrifices for their private ends ; and thus sacrifices to the gods have come down to the level of the private offerings made by an individual to his ancestors.

Still, however, the difference in might and majesty between a god and an ancestor deceased is retained and manifest in the Chinese religion, for Heaven, Thien, is ranked in the official hierarchy as supreme not only above the gods of the sun and moon and all other gods, but even above the ancestors of the Emperor : even in China, that is to say, the ancestors of the Emperor himself are not placed on a level with the supreme deity. The process of levelling up, however, has been carried on, and ancestor-worship has been exalted by various devices. Thus, the sun and moon, originally deities of their own right in China as elsewhere, are officially ranked as ancestors of the Emperor, that is to say, the worship of the Emperor's ancestors has been grafted on to the more ancient worship of the sun and moon ; and the Emperor himself officially takes rank as the son of Heaven. Again, an official combination, or contamination, of the worship of the gods with ancestor-worship has been effected in another way : elsewhere than in China there are rain-gods to whom, at the time when the rainy season is due, sacrifices for rain are offered, but in China on these occasions the sacrifices are offered both to the spirits of rain and thunder and also to the imperial ancestors. This tendency of the spirits of the dead to encroach on the domain of the gods is further illustrated by the fact that in China drought and the famine that ensues have come to be regarded at times no longer as due to the anger of the offended rain-gods, but as caused by the souls of the unburied, and therefore wrathful, dead. In the same way, the ceremonial of the offering of the first-fruits, which elsewhere is part of the worship of the harvest-gods, in China has come to be an offering to ancestral spirits. In other religions, again, and indeed in China also, animals are sacrificed to the gods, and when the gods have partaken of the offerings, the worshippers participate in the sacred meal, and by participating renew the bond of union between the community and its gods. In China the worship of the imperial ancestors has come to assume the rites and the form of the worship of the gods : a pig and goat are offered in the worship of the ancestors of the imperial house ; the ancestors are invited to partake of the sacrifice, and when they have partaken and have departed the remnants of the sacrifice are divided amongst the members of the family.

Another point, which shows the difference that even in China is felt and recognised to exist between ancestral spirits and the gods, comes out in connection with the tablets, containing the style and title of the deceased. It is before these tablets that offerings to the departed are made ; and at the State altars and in the State temples the gods also are represented not by images or idols of human shape, but by tablets—the object of this State-regulation being to assimilate the worship of the gods to ancestor-worship. But, in the thousands of temples to the gods, which are constantly frequented by tens of thousands of worshippers, the substitution of tablets for the anthropomorphic images of the gods has effected practically no hold. The difference between the tablets of deceased ancestors and the images of the gods, is the difference between ancestral spirits and gods ; and it is a difference which maintains itself in the popular mind, or common-consciousness, in spite of the attempts to blur it which have been made by the imperial house.

The offerings which are made to the spirit of the deceased were made originally to induce the ghost to go away and stay away ; and they consisted of the food and raiment which he might have need of in the next world, and for which, if they had not been properly buried with him, he might return to plague the living. The tendency, therefore, a growing tendency, is to increase the equipment of the dead. In order to propitiate the dead, to win their benevolence as well as to avert their male-volence, more and more things are buried with them, and come to be regarded as offerings made to them. In Athens this tendency reached such a pitch that it had to be stopped by Solon by means of a state enactment, limiting the amount and value of what might thus be withdrawn from the capital of the living. In China the tendency developed in the same dangerous direction, but the danger was counteracted by the Chinese—though not the peculiarly Chinese—device of " make-see " : in place of the food and costly raiment, the slaves and the concubines, and the money, which used to be buried or burnt with the deceased, paper slaves and concubines, gilt or silver paper in place of money, imitations of food and raiment in clay, straw, or paper are burnt.

Thus the making of offerings to the deceased is on the way to becoming a survival : the form is kept up, but, though maintained, it is only maintained ceremonially. On the other hand, the offerings made to the gods are real and substantial. And the reasonable inference from this difference between the offerings made to the dead and those made to the gods, is that from the gods the Chinese expect real and substantial benefits. If ancestors had substantial benefits to bestow, substantial offerings would be made to them. What maintains ancestor-worship in China is filial piety, much more than the hope of personal gain. Ancestor-worship is a duty, the first of duties, ranking next to the worship of the gods ; and it is disinterested, so far as disinterestedness is possible to human nature. The Chinaman honours his parents.

CHAPTER V

In none of the historic religions of the world is death conceived to be the termination of an individual's existence.

In Babylonia and Assyria, and amongst the Israelites, although religion was a bond rather between the community and the deity or deities than between the individual and his God, and although speculation on the future life was discouraged and even crushed, still the individual's existence was conceived to be continued in a shadowy manner after death. Where ancestor-worship flourished, as in China, or struggled on, as in Greece and Rome, the continuance of the individual after death is implied, even though the next life be pictured as vaguely and darkly as it was amongst the Israelites and in Babylonia and Assyria.

The aboriginal, or rather the pre-Aryan, peoples of India who have adopted Hinduism, in its various forms, are satisfied with the practical piety, *bhakti*, which it inculcates : conversion produces beatitude here and now, and a future life seems not to attract attention to itself. The Indo-Persians, ere

74

yet they separated from one another to enter India and Persia, seem to have developed a conception of the future life, according to which punishments and rewards awaited men in the next world. But whereas the Persians elaborated the conception and worked it out in such details as a resurrection, a last judgment, and a paradise, for Persians, and a hell, for everybody else ; the Aryan invaders of India allowed the conception to drop into the background to such an extent that it cannot be considered an important factor even in the religious system of the Vedas. In Brahminism it came to be displaced by belief in the transmigration of souls, *samsāra*.

The relative date at which this belief in transmigration was adopted into Brahminism is indicated by the fact that it makes its appearance in the older Upanishads ; but the source is quite uncertain. Amongst some of the aborigines of Australia the soul is believed to migrate from one human body to another, but such migration is not connected with any theory of punishment and reward. In Brahminism, however, the transmigration is conditioned by a primitive notion of retribution, and the bad soul is punished by being sent into the body of some animal, from which, however, it may subsequently return into the body of a man.

The crucial problem for Hindoo thought is how

escape is possible from this apparently interminable process of *samsāra*. To this problem Brahminism as a religion seems to provide no answer. As a philosophy it seeks the solution by means of a philosophical equation, in which the *ātmān*, or self, is identified or identical with Brahma, the sole and only reality ; and salvation consists in the release of the *ātmān* from the chain of existences.

Buddha felt the problem to be one of the utmost practical importance ; indeed, in his judgment the one and only question for man was how should he be delivered from the apparently endless chain of existences ; and he provided escape from the *samsāra* by the conception of Nirvâna. Whether Nirvâna was or was not to be understood as the cessation of existence was a point on which Buddha definitely and consistently refused to pronounce. His attitude on that question, and on other questions of capital importance for religion, such as the existence of God, was agnostic. His followers have been unable to maintain his attitude : they worship Buddha as God, and they regard Nirvâna not as the cessation of existence, but as the existence of the blessed.

From this brief survey of the attitudes towards the life to come that have been assumed by the various historic religions, it is clear that, though in none of them is death conceived to be the termination of an individual's existence, the amount of attention bestowed on the future life has varied considerably. In the various forms of Hinduism it is a subject which provokes little, if any, speculation. In China and in early Greece and Rome, where ancestor-worship developed, attention was concentrated on what the spirits of the deceased could do to harm or benefit the living, rather than on the fate and fortunes of the deceased themselves. In Babylonia and Assyria, and amongst the Israelites, religion was essentially conceived as an affair of the community rather than of the individual : it was between the community and its gods that the relation was held to consist, and not between any individual person and the god. And it was in this life that the bond between the community and its god existed, because it was in this world that the political community—which was the religious community—had its existence. In a small community, therefore, such as that of the Israelites, which had a hard struggle for national existence, that is, for existence as a political and a religious community, it was natural that energy should be concentrated on the practical task of surviving in this world, and should not be dissipated in speculation as to the fortunes of individuals in the next life.

Amongst the ancient Persians, who were also a practical people, and who were, moreover, a

conquering nation, there was, in consequence of
their conquests and political success, opportunity
and leisure to speculate on the next world. The
direction their speculation took was obviously
determined by the circumstances of their case.
Speculation as to the next world arose while the
Persians were still a closely-knit race and a conquering community : it was the closely-knit community
which had conquered in the struggle for existence
in this world—a struggle of the faithful band of the
worshippers of Ormuzd against the followers of
the evil principle who made up the rest of the population of the world—and it was the community which
would gain the victory over the followers of Ahriman
in the next world also.

As amongst the ancient Persians, so also amongst
the modern Mahommedans, paradise is reserved,
therefore, for those who are members of a particular
political community. The community is, indeed, as
seems to have been the case with all early political
communities, as much a religious as a political
community ; but, inasmuch as it was necessary
to belong to the political community in order to
be a member of the religious community, it was,
amongst the Persians, and is, amongst the Mahommedans, only by the extension of the political that
the religious community can grow. All men outside
the political community are unbelievers, and, as

such, are condemned to hell. In this respect the Mahommedan belief differs, in a fundamental and important manner, from that of Buddhism and that of Christianity. In the case of the two latter religions, the religious community is distinct from any political community, and is therefore, potentially, capable of becoming the universal religious belief of all mankind. In neither case is any man required to forsake the political community to which he belongs in order to become admissible to Nirvâna or to Heaven. Personal conviction and conversion are the requisites.

It is this requisition of personal conviction and conversion which marks the difference between the way in which the future life was envisaged in the religion of ancient Egypt, and that in which it is regarded by the modern religions of Buddhism and Christianity. In ancient Egypt speculation about the future life was worked out into minute detail and was translated into elaborate action, as the Pyramids and the Books of the Dead suffice to testify. But the basis of speculation in Egypt was different both from that of the ancient religion of Persia and from that of the modern religions of Christianity and Buddhism.

It was different from that of ancient Persia, in that the Persians, during their comparatively brief period of political conquest and national success,

became intensely conscious of the differences that
divided them from their foes, and never afterwards
lost that consciousness. It expressed itself in a
spirit of exclusiveness which rejoiced in the idea
that non-Persians were debarred from paradise
and doomed to hell. The ancient Egyptian, on
the other hand, does not seem to have troubled
himself with speculating about the latter end of
people who were not Egyptians : he was sufficiently
engaged in providing for his own future in the
next world. And this seems to indicate that speculation about the next world, and practical belief in it,
arose at a later stage of political and personal
development in Egypt than in Persia.

Persia was still one closely-knit political community, in which the individual counted himself
of little importance as against the State, when the
next world came to be regarded as the scene of the
ultimate triumph of the Persian community over
all the other peoples of the world. Egypt, however,
had already become an empire, fused of many
separate communities, each with its own local god,
or gods, before the belief in the next world assumed
the vivid form depicted on the monuments. Thus,
imperial Egypt became possessed of a pantheon,
and the bond between the individual Egyptian
and the gods generally was weakened, because his
religious attention was divided.

This relaxation of the bond it was that allowed the Egyptian to consider his own personal future in the next world, whereas the maintenance of the bond in Persia constrained the Persian to believe that, as in this life so in the next, his personal fate was bound up with that of the political community to which he belonged. What further impelled or assisted the Egyptian along this line of speculation and belief was the extent to which he pushed the use of magic. This, in itself an indication of the failure of the state religion to maintain its hold upon the individual, was what gave him his confident conviction that he could provide himself with the means of insuring his future in the next world. His existence, in the next life as in this, was conceived by him as depending on the preservation of his body : hence the care bestowed both on the mummification of the body, and on the preservation of the mummified bodies by the erection of. pyramids in which to bestow them. But as this method of preserving the body, on which the future life depended, was no absolute guarantee against its destruction, and was one which it was not in the power of the ordinary man to adopt, recourse was had to magic.

On the principle, fundamental in magic, of the substitution of similars, statuettes, representing the body of the deceased, would serve the same end

F

as the body itself ; and in the ratio in which they were multiplied, they gave the deceased an increased chance of continuing his existence in the next world. Nor was this the only utility of magic. The food, raiment, and other necessaries of existence in the next world, as well as in this, were, doubtless in Egypt as well as in other countries, originally buried with the deceased. But magical drawings of these objects would serve quite as well as the real objects themselves, and even better, inasmuch as they might be more lasting. Finally, by magic it was possible to ensure that the dead man would continue in the next world his occupation or enjoyment in this, for he had but to be represented as so acting and he would act so.

Thus the Egyptian view of the next world differed from the Persian, in that the Persian regarded it as the scene of the ultimate victory of the community, at once political and religious, to which he belonged, whereas the Egyptian regarded it as a place in which he would continue to enjoy earthly happiness. From the Buddhist and Christian conceptions it differed in that in them a personal conversion from the things of this world to a higher life is indispensable, whereas in Egypt it was not by religious conversion but by art-magic that the desired result was to be obtained.

It is true that even in Egypt religion was not

wholly driven from the field by magic. Admission
to the abode of the blest is always represented as
conditional. It depends on the ability of the
deceased to satisfy the judges in the next world
that he has led a moral life in this. Morality and
religion were felt by the Egyptian people, as by all
others, to be intertwined. But, though doubtless the
Egyptian's conception of the next world and future
happiness did strengthen his moral and religious
life, doubtless also his confident belief in magic did
much to mitigate the austerity of their demands.
Magic would not play such an important part in
the Books of the Dead, had not the Egyptian trusted
to it as much as he did to religion and morality.

The cardinal feature in the Egyptian conception
of the next world, as in the Persian and in the
Mahommedan, is that it is a state in which the
blessed continue to enjoy earthly goods. It includes
also punishment for the wicked. And this view
of the next life, as the scene of retribution, the place
of future punishments and rewards, is one which
at the present day is still widely accepted. The
demand for that justice which obviously is not
done in this world is so strong in the human breast,
indeed, that it is capable of being represented,
especially by a Utilitarian philosopher, as the real
reason for belief in a future life. From this point
of view our conviction that justice must ultimately

be done, if the universe is run on rational principles, is the sufficient reason for the belief in future punishments and rewards.

The assumption made in this appeal to our sense of justice is that the wrong-doer has gained in this world by his wrong-doing, and that retaliation in the next world is necessary to restore the balance, if justice is to be done. It is, however, precisely this assumption that by Christianity is called in question : what shall it profit the wrong-doer, if he gains the whole world and loses his own soul ? From this point of view additional punishment is presented as alike superfluous and impossible : crime will prove its own punishment.

That justice should be done on others—in the next world, inasmuch as it is not always done in this—is much more readily demanded than that it should be done on ourselves. Forgiveness for his trespasses is what a man prays for in his own case. And that demand is quite as deep-seated in human nature as the demand that justice should be done—on others. It appears in the Babylonian Penitential Psalms :—

> " Rend my sins, like a garment !
> My God, my sins are unto seven times seven.
> Forgive my iniquities."

But in Christianity the prayer may not even

be offered, unless the petitioner forgives others their trespasses against him. The mercy which he asks for himself he must first show to others. If what he desires for himself is not justice but love, what he must exhibit to others is something higher and more powerful than justice ; and that, in the Christian view, is love. On this view the two great commandments are that a man shall love God with all his soul, and his neighbour as himself. The next world, therefore, is not regarded as a clearing-house in which accounts run up in this life are settled, as it would be if the demand for justice were the sole, or the real, reason for belief in a future life. The Christian conviction that the Divine will is to be accomplished in every man, and that the perfect work of love will be fulfilled, is to the Christian the guarantee of future life.

It had not escaped the notice of the Greeks, of Aristotle, for instance, that there is something worse than suffering evil, and that is doing it. If, then, it is escape from doing evil that is desired, and nothing more, then, theoretically and logically, this end can be achieved by withdrawing from the world and from life. And this is the solution, essentially negative, which is proposed by Buddhism. By renouncing all his desires, a man is to cut himself off in this world from others, and from existence, the root of all evil, in Nirvâna. Thus, the Christian and the Buddhist views, both of this life and the next, differ from one another. In the Buddhist view, this life, or life itself, it is which is hell ; and escape from it, from this life, or from life itself, is what is sought. In the Christian view, this life is one in which it is possible for God's kingdom to manifest itself, and for His will to be done. The teaching of Christianity is positive, both as regards this life and the next : it is not merely that a man shall withdraw from the world and abstain from evil, or seek escape from life itself, but that he love his neighbour and his God and seek for eternal life.

The different views taken of the future life by the different religions of the world are naturally related to the various conceptions entertained of the nature and value of personality. Where, or when, the community's struggle for existence tasks or overtasks its strength, the loss of the individual counts little, if by it the community may survive : " to every man upon this earth death cometh, soon or late." And the god of the community, just because he is the god of the community, takes the community's view. A man has no standing before him save as a member of the community : in his individual, personal capacity, the man has no claim upon the god. And if he has none in this world, neither has he in the next. No claim was recognised, or even made, in the religions of Assyria, Babylon, or of the Israelites, or of the early Greeks and Romans : all men went down alike into the nether world.

Even where, as in the religion of the ancient Persians, the next world divides itself into a paradise and a place of torment, admission to the paradise may be conceived as conditional on membership of the community : it is in virtue of his membership rather than of his personality that the individual gains entrance, and the god is the god of the community rather than a being with whom the individual has personal relations.

The religions which longest maintained this conception that the god was the god of the community, and that the individual had no personal claim upon him, were the monotheistic religion of Israel and that of the Persians, which is rather to be described as dualistic than as a polytheism. Amongst the Hebrews, to the time of Jeremiah and Ezekiel, " the prevailing notions of religion had been national. Religion was a relation between Jahweh and His people, the Israelitish nation, rather than a relation between Jahweh and individuals ; and this had profoundly affected the conceptions of communion. It must have tended to cast a blight over the highest type of personal communion and piety."

Where, however, as in ancient Egypt, and in Greece when the Eleusinian mysteries developed, admission to future happiness depends on the individual's own acts, a distinct advance, if not in personality, then in the comprehension and realisation of it, is implied. It acts therefore with disintegrating force on the conception of religion as the relation of the community to its gods, and tends to bring forth the feeling that religion includes also the relation of the individual to the gods, and is not only a national but also a personal relation. It tends to expand the idea of God into that of a being who is concerned with the individual as well as the community. Man's conception of his own personality tends to grow as his conception of the Divine personality expands.

Man's conception of his own personality, however, may develop in two different ways. He may come to regard himself as an individual, and that individual may come to fill practically the whole field of his mental vision ; or he may come to realise more and more that as a person he is a member of a community, and that it is by and through his membership that his personality is both manifested and developed. His view of the next world will

naturally reflect, and perhaps magnify, his conception of his own personality. The ancient Egyptian
conceived that in the next world he was going to
achieve perfect happiness for himself, individually :
the community occupied no such place in his
vision of the next world, as the community of be-
lievers did in the vision of the ancient Persian, or
does in that of the modern Mohammedan. But
in all these three religions, in the Persian and
Mohammedan as well as in the Egyptian, the
attractions of paradise are a continuance of
earthly pleasures : heaven is a place wherein
man's will is to be done and the individual
is to enjoy himself. The conception of personality implied is that of a being who seeks his
own pleasure.

The Christian conception is that of a person who
loves others, his neighbour and his God, and who
seeks to do, not his own, but God's will. The
Christian conception of heaven accordingly is of a
state in which God's will is done. The value of
personality depends upon the extent to which the
person seeks to do God's will ; and the development
of personality upon the extent to which he does it.
He may wrap his talent in a napkin, or he may
invest it fruitfully in God's service, in which case
he will be called upon for further service, that is to
say, for further development of his personality,

and consequently a better comprehension of the Divine personality. And on the Christian view it is through love that this development of the human personality, and comprehension of the Divine, alone is possible.

CHAPTER VI

DUALISM

THE resemblances between Sanskrit and Persian, or Iranian, are so great, and the two form such a closely inter-related group in the family of Aryan or Indo-European languages, that the resemblances between the religions of the two peoples might be expected to be numerous and important also. But on examination this does not prove to be the case. For the libation made at sacrifices, the *soma* of the Hindoos, the Persians had etymologically the same word, *haoma*. The generic names for spirits or gods, which in Sanskrit are *deva* and *asura*, appear in Persian as *daéva* and *ahura*. But no proper, personal name for any individual god is common to the two languages ; and though the Hindoos, like the Persians who have been popularly known as fire-worshippers, also worshipped fire, a difference between the Hindoo worship and the Persian worship is undoubtedly indicated by the fact that the Hindoos used one word *agni*, the Latin *ignis*, for fire, and the Persians a totally different one, *átar*, which some scholars connect with the Latin *atrium*.

From this the probable inference is that the back-

ground common to the two religions contained
little, and probably nothing, more than spirits who
had not yet attained sufficient individuality to be
possessed of proper names, and to whom sacrifice
was offered, as it was offered by all communities in
the same early stage of religious evolution. It is
not, however, the back-ground common to the two
religions which is of interest to us here, but the
treatment which it received in Persia.

When a country is successfully invaded by a new
religion, the old gods are not immediately dismissed from being. Their existence is still recognised by the new religion, but their position is
altered. For those of them who are rooted too
deeply in the affections of the people to be dethroned entirely, some position in the new religion
is found by "accommodation," while the rest
continue to be recognised as existing, but are treated
as false gods, evil spirits and devils. That a new
form of religion did supervene in Persia upon that
which was inherited from the common ancestors of
the Hindoos and the Persians is disputed by no
one. Nor can it be disputed that the founder of
the new religion, Zarathustra, was a historical
personage. It is clear also that the old religion
accommodated itself to the new in Persia in much
the same way as was the case elsewhere. The fire-
worship of the old religion was continued in the

new ; and this result, though it points to the tenacity of the worship and its hold over the Persian people, was doubtless assisted by the fact that Zarathustra was a priest, engaged in the worship of fire. He retained fire-worship and even magnified its importance, making it to be, as it has ever since continued to be, the central rite in the Persian religion. He, like other religious reformers, apparently regarded himself not as founding a new religion, but as returning to the old faith. The fire, which was the hereditary cult-deity of his family, and of which he was a priest, was an *ahura*, a spirit or deity ; and in exalting that being, as Ahura Mazda (Ormuzd), he never proclaims it as a new god : he is evidently but restoring, as he imagined, the worship of the old. The orthodox conception of Ahura Mazda has always been that he is a flame radiating in uncreated light.

His work, however, of restoration, as he conceived it, carried with it the necessity of reform ; and the reform involved the necessity of putting an end to that worship of *daêvas* which had been inherited by the Persians from their Indo-Persian forefathers. In this reform he was supported by the dynasty of the Achæmenidae ; but, though the *daêvas* were thus deprived of worship, they continued to exist in the common consciousness of the Persian community, but to exist as false gods and devils. They came, in fine, to be degraded to

the level of the maleficent spirits, to whose malevolent attacks the ancestors of the Persians, like
other peoples in the same stage of evolution, conceived themselves to be exposed, and whom the
Persians termed *drukhs*.

Here, then, we have the source of that dualism,
in the religious sense, which is the characteristic
contribution of the Persians to the history of
religion. It is in its origin nothing more than the
division, drawn by most or all peoples in the earlier
stages of their religious evolution, between the
powers with whom the community has established
regular relations of worship, and those powers from
whom, as they are not worshipped by the community, the community has nothing but harm to
expect.

But, though in its origin the dualism of the
Persian religion is nothing more than this division,
it became much more in its development. To
understand its development, it will be well to pay
our first attention not to the power worshipped, but
to the powers from whom the community expected
harm and with whom it was consequently at war.
These powers were the *drukhs* and *devs*, numerous,
nameless, and united to one another by no other
bond than that of the common denomination of
daêva or *drukh*, and the common attribute of male-
volence and maleficence. Zarathustra himself, in

dealing with this element in the Persian dualistic system, or rather with these elements, did not regard them as manifestations of one concrete, personal being. We may reasonably conjecture that he was more immediately concerned to bring the Persians to class the *dâevas* whom their ancestors, and the ancestors of the Hindoos, had worshipped, as belonging to the same category as the *drukhs*. In the Gāthas, the older scriptures of the Persians, at any rate, theology did not advance further than to class both *daêvas* and *drukhs* as manifestations of evil. It is only in the more recent Avestas that the concrete, personal figure of Ahriman confronts us—the captain of the evil host.

If we now turn to the other element in the religious dualism of the Persians, we shall find that considerable difficulty is felt in determining whether the Ahura Mazda of Zarathustra and the Gāthas is to be regarded as a person and one god, or as " a monotheistic complex." The reason for regarding Ahura Mazda as a monotheistic complex is that he exercises his might and majesty by means of six beings, who are, as it were, hypostases of his qualities. These beings are the Ameshas Spentas, " the immortal holy ones." They are the spirits of fire, of earth, of water, of metals, of cattle and plants. If now we turn from these manifestations of the good principle in the Persian dualism, back to the evil principle, we shall find that the *drukhs* and *daèvas* stand to the evil principle, the *Ako* (*angro-*) *mainyu*, in the same relation as the Ameshas Spentas do to the *Spenta mainyu*, or good principle. And as some considerable time—the distance, whatever it may have been, that separates the Gāthas from the younger Avestas—elapsed before the evil principle, the *Ako* (*angro-*) *mainyu*, took concrete, personal shape in the figure of Ahriman, it may well have been the case that the good principle, *Spenta mainyu* or Ahura Mazda, was not at first a concrete personal figure, but only became so in the course of time and owing to a cause extraneous to the thought of Zarathustra.

Zarathustra's conception of the universe was that it is the scene of conflict between powers of good and powers of evil, of purity and uncleanness, of life and death. This dualism is, however, only an episode in the world-process : in the end—and here we reach the eschatology which was and still is characteristic of the Persian religion—truth and right will be victorious, all impurity and uncleanness will be done away, and there will be a new heaven and earth. The Ahura Mazda of Zarathustra is not a proper name : *mazda* is the Persian word for wisdom, and the conjunction of *ahura* with it indicates that wisdom is lord of all. The being of Ahura Mazda consists in absolute holiness, absolute purity and perfect justice. The justice, however, consists in retribution—a retribution which will be perfectly accomplished, in accordance with Zarathustra's eschatology, at the last day, evil for evil, and good for good. There was, therefore, in Zarathustra's scheme of retribution no place for either sacrifice or prayer ; of mercy and forgiveness there is no word. The supreme wisdom is not to be bribed by sacrifices, or to be cajoled by prayer. It is conceived juristically. The only term in the Avestas for " religion " is *daêna*—law.

Zarathustra's reform, then, was based on the fact that there are good and evil in the world, and on the conviction that in the end, at the last day, the good will be victorious. In the struggle between good and evil man is involved, and his ultimate fate will be determined by his action. It is by being pure, holy and righteous that man may advance the final triumph of the good ; and he will be judged at the last day in accordance with that " law," *daêna*, which for the Persian is " religion." It is by deeds of righteousness, of truth and justice, that a man will be saved : not by rites and sacrifices. Zarathustra's reformation, then, required the abolition of cult : sacrifices, rites and prayer were superfluous or were stumbling-blocks.

But the purity, which is one of the three qualities or constituents of the supreme wisdom, or Ahura

G

Mazda, permitted, and indeed developed, the purifications and atonements, which are the complement everywhere of the belief in taboo. Fire, earth, and water, to mention only three of the Ameshas Spentas, which went to make up the " monotheistic complex " of Ahura Mazda, all had to be guarded against impurity. They were all taboo and had to be protected from defilement. These taboos, inherited from the earliest times, were taken over by Zarathustra ; and to this day are observed by the Parsis as scrupulously as others still are by orthodox Jews. Fire must be extinguished in a house when a death takes place, lest it be defiled. It is defiled even if a vessel in which meat is being boiled should boil over. Water is sacred : a corpse may not be taken out for burial when rain is falling. Earth is polluted, if the corpse of a dead man or a dog touches it, and the field in which either is found must lie fallow for a year. Metals are similarly subject to defilement.

By including purity, then, as one of the three attributes of Ahura Mazda, Zarathustra recognised and sanctioned these taboos. As a fire-priest he started with the community's belief in the purity of that sacred element and in the necessity of protecting it from defilement. He was faithful also to the community's conviction that not only the spirit of fire, but the spirits of earth, of water,

dies, his body is dissolved into the various elements, the bones into earth, the blood into water, the life into fire, the hair into plants. On the last day the souls will reclaim all the constituent parts of their bodies, and each will rise, at the spot where he died, in full possession of all his individual qualities. Good and bad will arise at this resurrection, and will be separated, the former to go to heaven, the latter to hell. Then will there be great lamentation in the whole world, the good lamenting for the bad, the bad man lamenting for himself ; and the pain in the world will be like the pain of the lamb whom the wolf is devouring. Then will all the hills and mountains melt and pour over the earth, and all men must pass through the stream of molten metal. Through this ordeal will all men pass : to the just the glowing metal will prove to be as warm milk, to the wicked as a consuming fire. And, when this ordeal by fire is over, all men who survive it will live in unity and love, and with one voice will praise Ahura Mazda. Finally, the powers of good and of evil will engage in a last conflict. Ahriman and the evil host will be cast into the stream of molten metal. Then will the whole world be purified, the whole universe filled with Ahura Mazda's being, and all that lives will pass into immortality and celestial perfection.

The good who, at the last day, thus are justified

are the Persians. The bad, who are cast into consuming fire, are the rest of mankind. Plainly such a scheme can only recommend itself to the privileged community : it cannot commend itself to those outside the community. A religion of this kind cannot spread : it must and did shrink. Its dualism is its destruction.

CHAPTER VII

THE community by whom a god was worshipped was in all cases, save that of Buddhism, originally a political community ; and the worship was conducted in the interests of the community. The central religious rite, that of sacrifice, was accordingly in the hands of the ruler or of the ruling class, who were warriors. The greater, however, the importance attached to the proper performance of the rite, the stronger became the tendency for it to pass into the hands of a section of the ruling class, whose specialised function came to be that of acting as priests. Thus the governing class of the Aryan invaders of India came to consist of two castes, the Brahmins, or priestly caste, and the caste of Kshatriyas, or warriors ; and it is significant that Buddhism, as a revolt from Brahminism, was the work of a member of the Kshatriya caste, Gautama Buddha, who was born about B.C. 560 and lived to the age of about eighty.

When the founder of a new religion is a priest, as was Zarathustra, his mission presents itself to him as a reformation, and a return to the old ; and so too a prophet who is not a priest feels himself to be the mouthpiece through whom the god of the community chooses to speak. But Buddha neither felt himself to be the mouthpiece, or the prophet, of any god ; nor did he conceive his mission to be to reform, much less to restore, Brahminism. The message he came to proclaim was not to the Brahmins or to any one caste, but to all, of whatever caste, and of whatever political community, who had ears to hear. Distinctions of caste or of nationality he simply ignored. It is therefore not strange that he was without honour in his own country, and that Buddhism had to leave the land of its birth to do its work. The fact that it could do so and live shows that it possesses at least some of the qualities necessary for becoming a universal religion. Doubtless in China and Japan, neither ancestor-worship nor Shintoism satisfies the personal craving for religion. But that only shows that the soil was prepared : it does not explain the nature of the seed. To understand its nature, we must recognise that the appeal of Buddhism is practical and personal.

What is suffering ? what its origin ? and how shall man escape from it ? These questions come home personally and practically. They appeal to every man ; and if man were passive only, and not an active being, if he had capacity for suffering alone and not for action, a satisfactory answer to these questions might leave him with no more difficulties to propound, and Buddhism might become a universal religion. It is, however, only just where these are felt to be the sole practical personal questions that Buddhism is accepted : it has spread eastward from India but not westward. In India itself, the question, how man shall escape from suffering, was one of which the importance was magnified by the popular belief in the transmigration of souls, *samsāra*. In that belief death is no escape from suffering, for the man is reborn, it may be in animal form and to undergo yet worse suffering than he endured in human form ; and to this process no end is set, it is the unceasing revolution of a wheel.

It was, then, to a practical question, escape from suffering, that Buddha addressed himself ; and the first condition, as it appeared to him, for the solution of the question was to set aside gods and their worship. It was not necessary to deny them : it sufficed to ignore them. The rite of sacrifice, the central rite of the worship of the gods, had been developed—to excess—by the Brahmins, and the central fact of human existence, suffering, not only remained undiminished, it was not even touched. As a solution of the one practical question of life, belief in the gods was useless. And Buddha set it aside ; of man himself must salvation come.

The one goal is escape from suffering, and the path that leads to it must be trodden by man himself. Gods may be dismissed from consideration.

Buddha's teaching, then, was essentially non-religious ; and, if his followers had remained faithful to it, then Buddhism, however important in itself, would not be a religion : it would be no worship and have no god. But Buddhism is in truth a religion, for it has a god, a personal god. The foundation on which Buddhism rests is the personality of Buddha himself ; and that personality has, in the development of Buddhistic thought, been raised first to the ideal, and then to the divine, in spite of Buddha's attempts to divert the thoughts of his disciples from the worship of any god to their own personal escape from suffering. This fact it is which has converted Buddha's system of life into a religion. It is as worship, as worship of a god, that it becomes a religious force, and one of the religions of the world. But only by taking into the system of Buddha's thought an idea extraneous to it, the idea of God, has this been possible. That is to say, Buddhism, as a religion, is based on a principle which Buddha declined to assume. Escape from suffering, which is his object, remains that of his followers ; but, whereas he for its accomplishment taught that the gods might be waived aside, they have found by experience that to meet the needs of humanity a god is indispensable. Their faith is to believe—and to believe in Buddha, and the countless gods with whom the Buddhistic heaven has come to be filled.

Hence their religion, being based on faith and not on membership of any political community, is a missionary religion : to every man it is open to believe in Buddha. The mainspring of Buddhistic effort to convert mankind is sympathy and compassion—a brotherly love of all men. This democratic force it is which has made Buddhism a religion of the common people, and so has made it break entirely with the old conception of religion as an affair of the community mainly, or, as in ancestor-worship, of the family ; while it cuts at the root of magic—which exists, where it does exist, solely for the gratification of the desires of man—by its fundamental teaching that desire, even the desire to live, is the root of all evil.

The missionary force of Buddhism then is the sympathy and brotherly love which moves its followers to persuade all men to walk in the light of Buddha's truth, and to follow in his footsteps. For this, all that is necessary is personal conversion, and the resolve to follow the personal example set by Buddha himself. Thus, as being religious, Buddhism is the personal relation of a human person to a divine personality.

But though Buddha's followers have found the idea of God indispensable for the working of Buddha's system, and so have been compelled to use as a corner-stone the stone which Buddha himself rejected, still his object and purpose remains theirs. That object, however, it is important to note, is negative—it is the cessation of suffering—and its methods are negative : they are comprised in the prohibition, " abstain ! " As for the origin of suffering—and its source must be known, if suffering is to be made impossible—that is to be found in the desire for existence. The end to suffering, therefore, is to be found only in putting an end to desire. In that alone is salvation to be found. That is the sum and substance of what Buddha taught. " As the whole ocean is pervaded by one taste alone, the taste of salt, so is the teaching (of Buddha) pervaded by one taste alone, the taste of salvation."

The emotional basis of Buddhism is pessimism, the conviction that " all is suffering." And the pessimism is universal and radical. It is no mere recognition of the fact that in existence unhappiness, as well as happiness, may be found : it is the assertion of the principle that to exist is to suffer—existence is suffering and nothing else. Not only are sickness, old age, and death forms of misery, but birth and being alike are in themselves wretchedness. The water in the four great oceans is as nought compared with the tears men shed as they tread the path of life, and lament that what they loathe is the lot that falls to them, and what they love is no part of their lot.

For thorough pessimism of this kind, which will not suffer itself to be called in question, the conclusion is that the root of the whole evil is the desire to continue to exist. And the enormity of the evil was immensely magnified by the belief in the transmigration of souls, *samsâra*. It becomes necessary, therefore, to understand the part which *samsâra* plays in Buddha's system, and the modification to which *samsâra* was subjected by that system. To do so will be to see that, though Buddha was profoundly convinced that, for the solution of the practical problem of suffering, philosophy was just as superfluous and quite as misleading as religion, his system could no more dispense with a philosophical basis than it could work without the religious spirit.

His attempt to dispense with philosophy proves, on examination, to consist in attempting to substitute psychology for philosophy. The facts with which psychology deals are transient impressions and activities. With things in themselves psychology is not concerned, but only with our impressions. The external world, therefore, may be dismissed from consideration by psychology;

and, if we assume that psychology is right in dismissing them, and that there is no external world, then the impressions and activities with which psychology has to do are all that philosophy is concerned with. Every one of these impressions and activities—*sankhâras*—is an effect and a factor in a causal series, an effect of prior *sankhâras* in this or a previous existence, and the factor of future actions. Every act bears its fruit. That is the law—*dharma*—exemplified by everything that happens in the world. Thus the foundations of the metaphysics of Buddhism are the *sankhâras* and *dharma*.

But the central concept of Buddhistic thought is that of the *ātmān*, or self. The first point to be grasped, in endeavouring to understand this concept, is that it does not carry with it any assertion or implication that " I " exist or am in any way a reality. As has been said in the last paragraph, the only facts which psychology recognises, or with which philosophy, when it is identified with psychology, can deal, are transient impressions and activities. If it is supposed that the *ego* is anything over and above these impressions and activities, or underlying or distinct from them ; if it is imagined that " I " is anything more than a mere word used to sum up and indicate the totality of these impressions and activities, the reply is the

classical argument, used by Nâgasena to King
Milinda—that of the chariot. A chariot is made
up of its wheels, pole, and body. There is nothing
in the chariot over and above these constituent
parts, or underlying them or distinct from them ;
and as " chariot " is a mere word to sum up and
indicate the totality of its constituent parts, so too
" I " is a mere word and nothing more.

At death it is not merely the body which perishes,
but the " I " also, in the Buddhistic sense just
explained, must cease to exist. The impressions
and activities of the *ego* are transient, over and
ended as soon as begun, and the illusory " I " has
no existence, and never had any existence, apart
from them. But here it is that we come across the
philosophic conception or device whereby this
metaphysical argument is united to the doctrine
of *samsâra*, and, whereby the popular belief in the
transmigration of souls is reconciled with a metaphysical theory which seeks to dispense with the
very notion of a soul. The philosophic conception
used by Buddha to effect this junction is that of
karman. The activities which constitute the
illusory " I " result in deeds or work—*karman*—
and *karman* is not transitory, but permanent. It
survives the dissolution of the illusory " I," and
from the surviving *karman* are produced more
activities and a fresh individual whose life and lot

are determined by the *karman* of which he is the transient expression.

Thus the permanent and real is that which is done—the deed or work of the individual; and, if this seems to imply that the individual who does it is not a merely illusory " I," we may help ourselves out of the difficulty by remembering that to some Western thinkers it seems obvious that a man is what he does. This will enable us to pass from the metaphysics of Buddhism to its ethical system; for what a man does is either good or bad and must be either right or wrong. Thus in Buddhism the range or area of morality is enormously or indefinitely extended, for the quality of a man's actions determine his *karman* not only in his present form of existence, but in all subsequent forms. His morality or immorality shapes the *karman* not only for this life, but for all the future lives in which, on the doctrine of *samsâra*, it will manifest itself.

The popular form of the belief in *samsâra*, which Buddha found already in existence, was a belief in the transmigration of souls. But in the Buddhistic modification of the belief the soul plays no part. The " I " is illusory. A man is what he does, and what he does, the *karman*, it is which survives and passes on in *samsâra*. In the popular belief also no term was fixed to the process of *samsâra*.

Buddha's doctrine, however, was a gospel of salvation because it offered the prospect of escape from the wheel, and taught that it need not be a process which was endless. Buddha's teaching based itself on the position' that a man continues to exist because he desires to do so. The cessation, however, of his present existence, and the dissolution of the illusory " I," afford no escape from the wheel. So long as the desire of existence continues, there can be no cessation of existence : the *karman* will survive and the *samsâra* will continue to revolve.

If, then, escape from *samsâra* is to be found it can only be found in quenching the flame of desire. The abstinence from gratifying the various desires is but a palliative, for it implies that the desires are still there. What is wanted is to annihilate the desire for pleasure and the desire for existence altogether. The state in which desire is not quenched, but has ceased to be, the state to which the Buddhist yearns to attain, is Nirvâna. The way thereto begins with abstinence from gratifying the desires ; and the ethics of Buddhism consequently are essentially negative and consist of prohibitions. The first five commandments, incumbent on monks and lay brethren alike, are not to take life, not to steal, not to commit adultery, not to lie, not to drink intoxicants. The other five

H

commandments, which apply to monks alone, are also prohibitive merely.

The way of Buddhism begins with abstinence and leads to Nirvâna. Whether, however, the cessation of existence is ultimately implied, and so Nirvâna amounts to personal annihilation, is a point on which Buddha himself abstained from making any explicit pronouncement. And in Buddhism it is forbidden to discuss, or to seek to decide, between the alternatives of being and non-being, eternal and non-eternal, finite and infinite. All that can be said with certainty of Buddha's own conception of Nirvâna is that it is that state in which the *samsâra* is over and there is no more transmigration. This purely negative attitude towards the ultimate fate of man, however, was one which later Buddhism could no more maintain than it could maintain Buddha's purely negative attitude towards the idea of God. Indeed it was by renouncing the purely negative attitude that Buddhism became a religion. Accordingly, Nirvâna became definitely a state of blessed existence, and not a state in which consciousness has ceased to be, or may be supposed to have ceased. And Buddha himself became a god.

In other words, Buddha's followers learnt by experience that for a religion belief in personal immortality and belief in a personal god are indispensable. Buddha himself, however, evidently felt that neither for the explanation of the facts of life, nor for the practical regulation of the affairs of life, was it necessary to make any such assumptions. Existence was an evil, and escape from it was not facilitated by assuming the reality of personality, human or divine. On the other hand, an explicit denial of the reality of human personality would leave no one to exist or to seek escape from existence. Hence the assumption that " I " am an illusory existence. Hence also the difficulty that the " I " which does not exist should seek to escape from existence.

But though Buddha's followers had to abandon Buddha's negative views on personality, human and divine, Buddhism remains otherwise essentially a negative religion. The moral ideal of Buddhism is a peace of soul so perfect that it attains to absolute indifference, not only to pain and pleasure, but even to good and evil. The sympathy and brotherly love of Buddhism is consequently cooled down to the temperature of this absolute indifference. To the mother, lamenting for her dead child, the only comfort Buddha could give was to bid her see how every household had its sorrow, and know that " the dead are many and the living few." The attitude of the Buddhist monk is one of contempt for work, for women, and for all the conditions of active life. The objective of Buddhism is not to fit man for life, but to withdraw him from it. The first business of every man is by withdrawal from the world to seek his own personal salvation. The religious community exists in this world for the interest of the individual, and in the next world not as a community at all.

CHAPTER VIII

MONOTHEISM

Roughly speaking, we may say that at the present day the most highly civilised peoples are monotheistic, while polytheism generally goes with a lower stage of civilisation or barbarism, and amongst uncivilised peoples or savages a belief in spirits of some sort prevails. Again, roughly speaking, we may say that the history of the various forms of religion indicates that monotheism and polytheism were preceded by the worship of spirits. At first, the spirits worshipped are nameless. In course of time they come to be designated by the name of the object in which they are believed to manifest themselves—sun, moon, sky, wind, plant, or animal. Eventually, when the meaning of the designation comes to be forgotten and unknown, as, for instance, the derivation of Zeus and Jupiter from words originally meaning simply " sky " was unknown to the Greeks and Romans, the term becomes a proper name and stands solely for the personality which it has come to designate.

The inference suggested by these facts is that religion is a three-storied structure ; and that, while some people have never carried the structure higher than the first stage, that of polydæmonism, or belief in nameless spirits, most have added the second storey of polytheism, and some have crowned it with the third stage, that of monotheistic belief.

As against this inference, however, it may be argued that the original belief of man was in one God, and that polytheism and polydæmonism are errors from that original belief, and degradations of it. This argument does not necessarily come into conflict with the theory of evolution, for evolution is not synonymous with progress : all changes that take place are part of the process of evolution, but not all changes are progress or improvement from the point of view of man, or as judged by the standards which he employs. The changes which have taken place in religious belief may, possibly, in the past have been, in the case of all religious beliefs but one, at once phases in the process of evolution and departures from monotheism. The argument, therefore, that monotheism was the original religious belief, is not one which can be dismissed on purely *a priori* grounds. But neither is it one which can be admitted by the history of religions on purely *a priori* grounds. The history of religions is limited to historical facts and the inferences that can be drawn from them. For it, therefore, the question is, whether amongst the facts which it recognises and with which it deals there are any which indicate that monotheism is the earliest form of religious belief that it can discern.

The existence amongst low races of a belief in high gods is a fact for the establishment of which the science of religion is indebted, as it is for many other things, to Mr Andrew Lang. It is precisely amongst savages, who were supposed not to have risen above the worship of nameless spirits, or not even to have attained to any religious belief whatever, that Mr Lang demonstrated the existence of a belief in beings who are not anonymous but in possession of personal names, and who are high gods both in their dignity and in the fact that they are exalted above all worship. The suggestion that the conception of such high gods was really borrowed from early missionaries or explorers is one which Mr Lang has satisfactorily rebutted. We may safely take it that the conception is native to the lands in which it is found.

The question is, what the inference may be which it is legitimate to draw from these facts ; and the first thing we notice is that, as Mr Lang himself recognised, the belief in these high gods, where it occurs, does not in the least indicate that the savages who hold it are monotheists. The aborigines of Australia, who have several of these high gods, or " all-fathers "—Daramulun, Baiamai,

Twanyinika—are certainly not monotheists. The West Africans, who have their Anyambĕ, are polytheists. The Unkulunkulu of the Zulus cannot be described as their one and only god. These high gods are figures that are found side by side with forms of polytheism or polydæmonism, even if they do not belong to them. What, then, is the inference to be drawn from this juxtaposition ? It may well be that the figures of these high gods, standing out from the low growth of polydæmonism or polytheism that surrounds them, are survivals from an older period. The fact that they have personal names proves that they are figures of some antiquity. We may even indulge in the conjecture that they are survivals from a period of belief in one God alone. But against this conjecture there are several points to be taken into account.

It would seem strange, first, that the memory of primitive monotheism should have been preserved down to the twentieth century by the negroes of Africa, the black fellows of Australia, or casual tribes in Patagonia ; and that it should have disappeared, for we may safely say that it was absent, from the minds of the ancestors of the Indo-European peoples three or four thousand years ago.

Next it is to be noted that these " all fathers," or high gods, are not worshipped, even where the spirits or polytheistic gods by whom they are surrounded receive worship. If, then, we regard it as an essential and distinguishing characteristic of these high gods that, as at the present day so from the beginning, they received no worship, we are forced to the conclusion that the primitive monotheistic deity had no worshippers. If, on the other hand, we regard it as part of the meaning of the term " god " that he is a being worshipped by man, then we shall hold that these high gods weie once, though they no longer are, worshipped ; and we shall reject the native West African explanation that he never did receive worship, just because he never was imagined to take any active interest in the affairs of man.

By adopting this view, that these high gods were at one time worshipped, we are enabled to descend from the heights of *a priori* speculation to the facts which the history of religions affords us. The question as it now presents itself to us is whether in the history of religions we come across cases in which a god, who was once a member of an ordinary polytheistic pantheon, comes to be no longer an object of worship but simply a survival, and a name honoured indeed but forming no practical part of the religion of the community ? Now, that is in the Vedas precisely the case with the ancient *Dyâus Pitar*, " father sky " : of his original brilliance there remains but the faintest glimmer in the Vedas.

Like the Anyambĕ of the West Africans he does nothing and he receives no cult. Other deities have come to receive the worship which once was his, and he remains but a name. He with other " high gods " remains respected, and therein their case differs from that of other gods who have elsewhere been dethroned more roughly. They are relegated by the invading religion in such cases to the position of false gods, as, for instance, in Persia the *dêvas* came to be *daêvas*.

It seems, therefore, quite possible for the history of religion to account for the scattered occurrence of the high gods by means of the fact that survivals occur in the evolution of religion as well as in the evolution of bodily organisms. And this seems preferable, at present, to resorting to the *a priori* assumption of a primitive monotheism.

But, even if we decide to regard these high gods as furnishing little or no presumption that low races have preserved to the twentieth century traces of monotheism which had disappeared thousands of years ago from the consciousness of the ancestors of the Indo-European peoples, we have yet to consider how the question is affected by the case of the Israelites. From the point of view of Comparative Religion we are debarred from assuming that the religion of the Israelites stands in absolute isolation from all other religions, and that it has no points of resemblance to them whatever but only points of difference. We are also equally debarred by the Comparative Method from assuming that the religion of the Israelites is just like that of any and every other religion, and has nothing characteristic or unique about it. We may recognise that every tree has trunk, boughs, and leaves, and yet hold to the plain fact that oak-leaves are not to be found on birch trees, nor chestnut branches on a poplar ; the very likeness of one species to another implies an unalterable difference between the two. Comparison, though revealing resemblances, will also reveal differences in the very point of resemblance ; leaves are leaves, but the leaves of the chestnut are different from those of the silver birch. And though the differences between things may become more minute the further back their history is traced, still it is obvious, and is coming to be recognised in science, that even the molecule, or atom, or whatever is for the time regarded as the ultimate element, cannot be regarded as homogeneous in its constitution : out of the homogeneous the heterogeneous cannot come.

We may therefore expect that what can be discerned of the Israelitish religion in pre-Mosaic times will have its resemblance to other forms of religion, and will show its differences in the very point of resemblance. Resemblance is manifest in the fact that the central rite of worship was the sacrificial rite, in the Israelitish as in all other early communities. The sacrifice was offered to the god of the community, here as elsewhere, on behalf of the community by the head-man of the community. The god was reverenced as protecting his worshippers from calamity ; or, if he suffered it to come upon them, it was because some member of the community had offended against him. Thus the conduct which it was the custom of the community to display and to expect to be displayed, and the offences which it was its custom to condemn, were regarded as actions which met with the god's approval or disapproval ; morality is compliance with the will of the god. That death did not terminate the individual's existence, even if he went down into the grave and were no more seen, was as self-evident in the eyes of the pre-Mosaic Israelites as it was to every other people. Circumcision, which is practised not only by tribes in Asia and Africa, but by tribes in Central America, South America, the Malay Archipelago, the New Hebrides, and Australia, is a rite which evidently—whatever its origin and significance—goes back in the history of the Israelites to a time when they were at least as remote from civilisation as any of the savages who practise it to-day.

If, then, in imagination, we transport ourselves

to the time when the ancestors of the Israelites were in that stage of evolution in which circumcision is regarded as incumbent upon every one who is to become a member of the community, and as the badge of all the tribe, we shall be prepared to admit the possibility and the probability that other resemblances also may have existed between the Israelites and tribes in that stage of their evolution. Circumcision goes back, we may reasonably imagine, to a time when the name Jahveh had as yet not come into existence, and when the god, who protected the community and was worshipped with sacrifice, had not yet acquired a proper, personal name.

If now we employ the Comparative Method and compare the religion of the Israelites with that of other branches of the Semitic race, we shall find that one other branch, the Phœnicians, even when they had become pronouncedly polytheistic, still adhered to the primitive method of designating the deity by a general term rather than by a personal name. Among the Phœnicians, the ordinary term for deity is Ba'al, that is to say, the lord and master who owns the land and rules the tribe, and is the protecting deity of both. Every Phœnician community had its Ba'al whom it worshipped ; and each local Ba'al came to be distinguished from every other by the addition of the name of the community by whom it was worshipped, *e.g.* the

Baʿal of Tyre or Sidon or Tarsus, and his power did not extend beyond the limits of the locality of which he was the owner or beyond the community of which he was the lord. Even when, as came to be universally the case amongst the Phœnicians, other deities with personal names came to be worshipped by the community, the Baʿal still remained the highest god. The inference, then, is that the Baʿal remains the highest god because he was first in possession ; and that each locality or community originally knew the object of its worship merely as its lord and master, Baʿal, and not by any proper, personal name.

Some of the steps by which the Phœnicians, Canaanites, and Syrians, starting from the worship of the nameless deity whom his worshippers knew simply as their lord and master, their Baʿal, developed this worship into polytheism, are plain to us ; and the operation of these causes is not limited to the area of Semitic religion. Thus, the *numina* of the old Italian religion, though personalised very imperfectly and anthropomorphised but slightly, came early to be classed in pairs, as male and female. But, owing to their imperfect personalisation, their relations to each other were not worked out anthropomorphically : they were not conceived as constituting families, or a community. And though to these pairs of divinities the names "father" and "mother" were given, the names did not imply conjugal relationship between the pair, but indicated that they were *numina* on whom the protection of the community and the fertility of its human members and of its cattle depended. In the same way, and owing to the same causes, the non-Israelitish Semites came to differentiate the nameless deity whom they worshipped into a Ba'al, or lord or master, and a Ba'alat, or lady and mistress. The worship of such a Ba'alat, under the name of Astarte or Ishtar, came to be one of great importance first in Babylonia and Assyria, and then throughout the ancient world.

Another cause, not limited in its working to the Semitic race, which operated among the non-Israelitish Semites to develop the worship of the nameless deity in the direction of polytheism, was the tendency of the human mind to imagine that where there are two names there must be two objects to correspond to them. The deity worshipped generally as Ba'al could also be described as lord or king ; and such cult-epithets, in all religions, have a tendency eventually to be conceived as indicating the existence of distinct deities corresponding to the distinct epithets. Thus, we may reasonably suppose, the terms '*Adôn*, lord, and *Melek*, king, as used at first, were simply alternative designations of the deity more commonly and generally spoken of as Ba'al. They then came by use and wont to be cult-epithets ; and eventually the different cult-epithets came to be understood as designating different objects of worship and deities distinct from one another.

What distinguishes the Israelites from the other branches of the Semitic race is the tenacity with which they clung to the worship of the god of their own community, their own peculiar lord and master, and refused either to discriminate him into a Ba'al and a Ba'alat, or to be misled by the fallacy that lurked in the use of cult-epithets. Their deity was, like all other deities, originally nameless. He came indeed to have a proper name, Jahveh ; and this served, or perhaps proved necessary, to distinguish him and the community that worshipped him from other Semitic tribes with their Ba'alim. But to distinguish two objects is to acknowledge that they admit of comparison. In this case it was to admit that the gods of the heathen were also, as well as Jahveh, gods ; and the assertion that he was a god above all other gods was still an admission that the others were gods. The impossibility and the illogicality of such an admission came eventually to be felt and to be expressed with sublime scorn in the assertion that, as for the gods of the heathen, they are but idols. But it is not felt or expressed in the central or fundamental conviction of the Israelites that Jahveh is the God of Israel, and Israel is His people. Such a religion is tribal ; the worship of Jahveh cannot be universal, any more than can the worship of Ahura Mazda be ; nor could it even attain the potentiality of becoming universal until it ceased to be the worship of Jahveh. A god with a personal name remains one of a class, one god among many ; polytheism is recognised, and, in proportion as it is recognised, monotheism is imperfectly developed.

If, then, the worship of Jahveh is to be regarded as an imperfect form of monotheism, the form of worship which preceded it must have been one which, even though monotheistic, was still less developed. It was one in which the deity worshipped by the community had no personal name, but was addressed in some such manner as that of the Phœnicians, by the term, lord, or, as in one of the local cults of ancient Egypt, by the designation of "dweller in the west" (Chentamentet). But so long as the deity of the tribe has no proper name, but is simply the lord or master, he can take over every function of deity as it comes to be recognised as such. The importance of this consideration is that, as no deity starts his career with a proper name, there can at the start be no practical question of polytheism or monotheism.

To treat religion, therefore, metaphorically, as a

I

structure, and to suppose that originally it was a one-storied structure of polydæmonism to which some peoples added a second storey of polytheism, and some a third storey of monotheism, is to be led astray by an inappropriate metaphor. We must rather conceive the relation of men to their gods, which is religion, as at the beginning capable of being interpreted as the relation of the community to a spirit. There is nothing in the facts with which the history of religion deals to compel us to assume that every community started with a belief in a plurality of vaguely conceived spiritual beings ; and there is the case of the Israelites, a people singularly tenacious of beliefs and customs, such as the custom of circumcision, which it has retained from a period of very primitive barbarism, to show us that the belief in a single, nameless, spiritual being may go back as far as we can trace or surmise their religious evolution. On the other hand, the differentiation of the vague concept of a being that is worshipped into several beings, is probably the result of a slow process rather than a single act achieved at one blow : as long as the beings were nameless there would be difficulty in differentiating them and keeping them distinct. In any case, however, it seems misleading to apply the terms polytheism or monotheism to a stage of religious evolution so little developed as this. All that it seems safe to say is that it was a stage from which it was possible for either polytheism or monotheism to evolve. We may say that, and yet hold it probable that the line of evolution which was to lead to polytheism diverged at a very early moment from that which led to monotheism.

It is part of the connotation of the term "god" that a god is a being who has, or has had, worshippers. From the point of view of the Christian believer in monotheism, therefore, who holds that there is but one God of all the world, it follows, on the one hand, that all men, so far as they have worshipped in truth and in spirit, have, little as they may have known it, worshipped the one God; and, on the other hand, that the God, after whom they have ignorantly sought, is to them as yet a God unknown, or misconceived. From this point of view, therefore, the worshippers of the one God are potentially, but not actually, all men. What is implied for the monotheist by the connotation of the term "God" is that the community of His worshippers, actual and potential, is co-extensive with mankind. The conversion of potential into actual worshippers is a function exercised by Christianity as a missionary religion.

The concept, therefore, of the community of worshippers tends, as monotheistic religion develops, to extend beyond the limits set to it at first. In the earliest form, that of the Israelites, the community of worshippers consists of the national and political community ; and in Mahommedanism the same restriction holds good. Neither form therefore in this respect seems capable of becoming perfectly monotheistic : the God, indeed, in both religions is one, but neither is a proselytising religion. It is a popular error to imagine that the Muslim conqueror offers to the conquered the alternatives of death or conversion to Mahommedanism. The holy war of Mahommedanism has for its purpose not to convert non-believers, but to destroy their political power. Whether the conquered choose or not to become Mahommedans is their affair : it is not a process which the conqueror cares to promote. On the contrary, he usually discourages it.

Of Christianity, however, it is the distinguishing characteristic that it seeks to draw all men to it. This difference between Christianity and the two other less highly evolved forms of monotheism implies a profound difference between them in their attitude towards personality. The conviction that Jahveh is the God of Israel, and Israel is His people, is one which does not recognise that the individual members of the community have any claim to appear personally before the Lord : their existence as persons is not recognised. The rite of sacrifice was performed on behalf of the community as such, and not on behalf of its members personally. The rite was therefore an obstacle to personal religion.

In Mahommedanism this obstacle is done away : sacrifice is no longer a rite practised or recognised. Prayer takes its place ; and if prayer, as understood by Mahommedanism, *salāt*, were what Christianity understands by it, the difference between the attitudes of the two forms of monotheism towards personality would be less. But *salāt* is a rite depending for its efficacy on the correct and punctilious performance of the ritual, not on the spiritual disposition of the person praying. Its purpose is praise and thanksgiving. When it proceeds to petitions, they are for the deliverance of the community from its misfortunes, not for the deliverance of the individual from personal temptation and evil. Worship in Mahommedanism is a function of the community, as it is in all religions ; but it does not go further. It does not require the worshipper's personal communion with his god, still less does it admit of the idea that all men are the object of Allah's love and care : non-Mahommedans are enemies of Allah and his people, and against them it is the religious duty of the faithful to conduct a holy war of extermination.

The value, then, of personality is rated low in

those religions which make membership of a political community indispensable for the faithful. Those outside the community are regarded with a disdain and contempt which permits of their treatment, and, when occasion offers, incites to their treatment, as beings who have no claim to be respected as persons or even to be regarded with compassion as human. Those inside the community are valued not as persons, or as ends in themselves, but as means by which the community's ends may be attained. This low estimate of personality, both within and without the limits of the community, is characteristic alike of the Jewish and the Mahommedan forms of monotheism ; and it marks them as imperfect evolutions of this form of religion. Monotheism is essentially a personal religion, in that it is a personal belief in a personal God. Its evolution, therefore, is a process in which the personality, both of the believer and of his God, becomes more and more manifest ; and that process is evidently impeded, if not arrested, by everything which depreciates the value of human personality. Where human personality is valued low, as it must be in a religion which exists to promote the interests of a political community, the concept of divine personality cannot be of the highest. And, on the other hand, it is only where the conception of the divine personality is of the highest that human personality is valued at its proper rate, and that the saving of even one sinner that repenteth can be felt to be a cause of the highest rejoicing. The community that so rejoices is one which has advanced further on the lines of personal religion than is possible for those forms of monotheism which, because they are less perfectly monotheistic, fail to attain to a full recognition of the worth of personality.

In those forms of religion in which sacrifice is the central rite of worship, it is for the community that sacrifice is offered : the end proposed is to avert calamity from the community and to ensure its earthly prosperity. And the gods are consequently relegated to the position of means to the end, just as are the individuals who compose the community. If, in such a form of monotheism as the Jewish, the deity is exalted in transcendent majesty above the community, the personality of its members is but reduced in value, and the idea of the possibility of personal communion is one which the official religion cannot encourage. For the recognition of the value of human personality as an end in itself there is no scope ; and the reason of this is to be sought in the fact that the divine personality itself is treated as a means to the community's ends. The form of monotheism which regards persons as not only means, but as themselves ends, is the

Christian religion ; and it is enabled so to regard them by the conception or conviction that God is love. The conception of a person as both the subject and the object of love is one which raises the value of personality, both human and divine, and makes it an end without ceasing to regard it as a means.

The Christian conception of love—of God's love for man, and man's love for his neighbour and his God—is one which gives a new meaning, and for the Christian gives the true meaning, of personality, the community and worship. It is, philosophically, a new view—a view which had never been entertained before—of the relation of man to God, that is to say, of religion. It is, practically, a new direction given to the method of experiment, by which men at all times of their history have been endeavouring to work out the problem of the relation of man to God. We may say even that the power of love, as understood by Christianity, is a new force. But in saying so we must lay stress on the qualification that it is love as understood by Christianity which is a new factor in the endeavour to work out in practice the practical relation of man to his neighbour and his God.

It is necessary to emphasise the qualification in order to understand the position of Christianity in the history of religion, that is to say, in order to understand those resemblances and differences between Christianity and other forms of religion, which are presupposed by the very attempt to apply the Comparative Method to them and to bring them within the scope of the study of Comparative Religion.

For thousands of years before the appearance of Christianity on earth, wherever and whenever a community of human beings was to be found, man must have had some love for his fellow-man : no community could have held together had it been absolutely and totally wanting. But, though we can infer its existence, the very fact that we resort to inference suffices to show both that the consciousness of it as an operative force was dim, and that there were other operative forces at work. In the struggle for existence, self-preservation, and the defence of the community, which was also self-defence, was, in a sense, the first law of nature. Even though some love, however small and unconscious, for the other members of the community must have existed, if the community was to hold together at all, no love for members of a strange community was entailed.

Some love for the gods they worshipped, and to whom they appealed for the protection and the prosperity of the community, is implied in the existence of the feast of sacrifice, of which both the god and his worshippers partook. But it is equally obvious from the history of all religions in which sacrifice is the central and essential ceremony that it was neither on the love of the worshippers for their god, nor on his love for them, that they consciously relied, but on the due performance of the rite and on the due fulfilment of the contract implied.

Thus, though by digging below the surface we discover that love—love for a man's neighbour and for his God—must have been operative to some extent from the beginning, and that, so far as it was operative, there is a resemblance, and indeed an inner bond, between Christianity and other forms of religion, we are compelled also to recognise that the difference is great between the unconscious love which we infer to have existed in the one case, and the love proclaimed as the central truth and the guiding principle in the other. The difference is great, and its magnitude may be measured—from the outside —by the revolution it effected in the conceptions of worship, the community, and the personality of God and man.

Where worship centres in the rite of sacrifice, the rite is indeed the means whereby the community is brought into the presence of its lord ; but it is also a veil which is drawn between the individual worshipper and his god ; and so long as sacrifice may only be offered by or on behalf of the com-

munity, as was the case in Israel, it is a veil beyond
which an individual member of the community
may not penetrate, for as an individual and as a
person he has no position or standing in the community's religion. The veil may indeed come to
be regarded as itself the one and only substantial
reality, as in Brahminism, where religion and the
gods themselves are swallowed up in sacrifice. On
the other hand, where, as in most other ancient
religions, the individual members of the community
are not content to be excluded from the rite of
sacrifice and to be debarred from coming with their
individual petitions before the god, there grows
up the practice of private sacrifices for private ends,
or the individual resorts to the use of magic. In
either case the outcome is one of deteriorating effect
upon the worshipper and his conception of the
relation between God and man. Magic must be
resorted to, where the end desired is one which is
condemned by the community as anti-social and
irreligious ; that is to say, it encourages the person
employing it to imagine that he can succeed in
opposition to the dictates alike of morality and of
religion ; and so it fosters the growth of a type
of individual whose existence and activity are injurious, and would, if unchecked, prove fatal to the
community.

Private sacrifice is more subtly dangerous even

than magic, for, save amongst the Jews, the danger
went unnoticed : magic is readily condemned by
the religious sentiment, but private sacrifice, except
amongst the Jews, goes uncondemned. So long
as sacrifice is offered solely on behalf of the community, self-love is excluded as a motive. But
when private sacrifice for private ends comes first
to be permitted, and then to be recognised as a
religious rite, the relation of men to their gods,
which is religion, is substantially altered for the
worse. Sacrifice tends to be regarded as a bargain,
based on the principle of *do ut des* ; and self-love
comes to be felt to be the only rational motive for
offering sacrifice. Thus the character of both
parties to the transaction is dishonoured : the god
is lowered to the level of a party to a commercial
transaction, and the only human motive that is
supposed to act, or to be capable of acting, is self-
interest. When this is the case, the spirit of worship,
which originally breathed through the rite of
sacrifice, has obviously evaporated ; and though
the rite may be preserved by " the cake of custom,"
its religious significance has departed from it. For
a ceremony which either excluded the members
of the community as persons in their own right,
or only admitted them on terms dishonouring alike
to the human personality and the divine, Christianity
found no place in its system. A system based on

the love of man for his neighbour and his God is one which provides no place for self-love. The ritual offering of sacrificial animals ceases to have any religious significance for a religion which proclaims worship to be spiritual, and understands by the term sacrifice the offering of a broken spirit and a contrite heart.

The conception of the community which, by offering sacrifice, worshipped its God was correspondingly changed in Christianity, and the content of the concept was both transformed and enlarged. So long as the concepts of "sacrifice" and "worship" were not differentiated but apprehended or misapprehended as one confused category, it was possible, and, as the history of religions indicates, inevitable that the circle of worshippers should be regarded as exactly co-extensive and conterminous with the community that actually joined in the offering of the sacrificial victim, or, as the community enlarged, with the tribal or political community which offered sacrifice to the same deity. In either case the circle of worshippers was limited and confined to those who joined in offering animal sacrifice ; and a religion thus cabined and confined to a tribal or political community was debarred by its very nature from spreading beyond those confines and becoming a universal religion. But when the terms " sacrifice " and " worship " came to be differentiated by Christianity, the intension and the extension of the term "worshipper" were transformed and enlarged. The intension was transformed because the meaning of the term was disclosed to be that it signified a spiritual relationship; and the extension was enlarged because it was realised that the term was one which by its very meaning was capable of being extended to every man, bond or free, Jew or Gentile, who desired to enter into that relationship.

But the Christian conception of worship transformed the conception of the community still further. In all the religions of the world the community had always been regarded as comprising both the gods and men. The sacrificial feast was one of which both the god and his worshippers partook; the rite was one in which the worshippers appeared before their lord. As polytheism grew, however, the tendency manifested itself to regard the gods as forming a community of their own, and as being more, or much more, interested in its affairs than in the affairs of men. Sacrifice remained indeed a link between men and the gods, but it ceased to be a spiritual bond in proportion as it came to be regarded as the making of offerings for the purpose of obtaining favours in return. A link so weak, and so offensive to the religious sentiment, was apt to break, with the result of completely segregating

the gods from man : gods and men no longer formed
one community. The sacrificial rite was no longer
capable of holding them together. By the Christian
doctrine that God is love and that man shall love
his neighbour and his God, the community of
worshippers is transformed potentially into that
kingdom of God, the coming of which is the first
petition in the Lord's Prayer. The community of
worshippers is rooted in communion with God ;
and it is capable of extension so as to include every
man. The God, with whom communion is sought,
no longer by means of the sacrificial rite, but by a
spiritual worship, in which every member of the
human race may share, is no longer a tribal or a
national deity, but the God of all the world.

The relation of men to their gods, which everywhere is what is implied by religion, is one which
is interpreted, and is in practice worked out in a
different way in every different form of religion.
The different forms of religion might even be said
to be the different ways in which the relationship
is acted on. Where the relation is conceived to be
one existing between the community and its god,
it is the community that has access to the deity
worshipped by sacrifice : the members are not
distinguished or recognised as persons. Where
private sacrifice comes to be usual, or where magic
is tolerated, the relation of men to their gods is

profoundly affected by the tendency to treat the gods in practice as means to the ends which the individual happens to desire. Thus self-love is not only taken up into the conception of personality : it tends to become the dominant feature in the conception of personality and its mode of action.

The interpretation, however, which Christianity puts upon the conceptions of worship and the community is but an expression of its different conception of personality, divine and human, a conception peculiarly its own. A spiritual worship and a community from which self-love is excluded imply an ideal of personality unknown to other forms of religion. The perfect personality of the Christian religion, regarded from the human side, is an incarnation of the divine love, while of the divine side the conception is that God is love. Love is the perfect expression of personality because it is, on the Christian view, the core of personality.

BIBLIOGRAPHY

ACHELIS, T. *Die Religion der Naturvölker.* 1909.
—— *Vergleichende Religionswissenschaft.* 1908.
BARTH, A. *Les Religions de l'Inde.* 1870.
BOUSSET, W. *What is Religion?* 1907.
BRINKLEY, CAPT. *Japan, its History, Arts and Literature.* London. 1904.
BUDGE, E. A. W. *The Book of the Dead.* 1898.
—— *The Mummy.* 1893.
CAIRD, E. *Evolution of Religion.* 1899.
CAMPBELL, L. *Religion in Greek Literature.* 1898.
CHANTEPIE DE LA SAUSSAYE, P. O. *Religionsgeschichte.* 1905.
CROOKE, W. *Popular Religion and Folk-Lore of Northern India.* 1896.
CUMONT, E. *The Mysteries of Mithra.* 1903.
DE GROOT, J. M. *The Religion of the Chinese.* 1910.
—— *The Religious System of China.* 1892-1901.
FARNELL, L. *Greece and Babylon.* 1911.
—— *The Higher Aspects of Greek Religion.* 1912.
GURU PROSAD SEN. *An Introduction to the Study of Hinduism.* 1893.
HAUG, M. *Religion of the Parsis.* 1884.
HOPKINS, E. W. *The Religions of India.* 1895.
JACKSON, W. *Zoroaster.* 1899.
JEVONS, F. B. *The Idea of God in Early Religions.* 1910.
JASTROW, M. *The Religion of Babylonia and Assyria,* 1898.
—— *The Study of Religion.* 1901.

K

KERNS, H. *Manual of Indian Buddhism.* 1896.

LYALL, A. C. *Asiatic Studies.* 1884.

MASPERO, G. *Histoire ancienne des peuples de l'orient Classique.* 1895.

MAX MÜLLER. *Origin and Growth of Religion, as illustrated by the Religions of India.* Hibbert Lectures. 1878.

MONTEFIORE, C. G. *Origin and Growth of Religion, as illustrated by the Religion of the Ancient Hebrews.* Hibbert Lectures. 1892.

OLDENBERG, H. *Buddha, sein Leben, seine Lehre.* 1897.

Religious Systems of the World. A Collection of Addresses. 1905.

ROBERTSON SMITH, W. *Kinship and Marriage in early Arabia.* 1885.

RHYS DAVIDS, T. W. *Buddhism.* 1877.

SANDAY, W. *Personality in Christ and in Ourselves.* 1911.

SAYCE, A. H. *The Early History of the Hebrews.* 1897.

—— *Lectures on the Origin and Growth of Religion.* 1888.

SELL. *The Faith of Islam.* 1896.

SMITH, S. G. *Religion in the Making.* 1910.

TIELE, C. P. *Science of Religion.* 1897.

WARDE FOWLER, W. *The Religious Experience of the Roman People.* 1911.

WEBB, C. C. J. *Natural and Comparative Religion.* 1912.

WHITTAKER, T. *Priests, Philosophers and Prophets.* 1911.

WILLIAMS, M. *Modern Hinduism.* 1887.

—— *Religious Thought and Life in India.* 1883.

INDEX